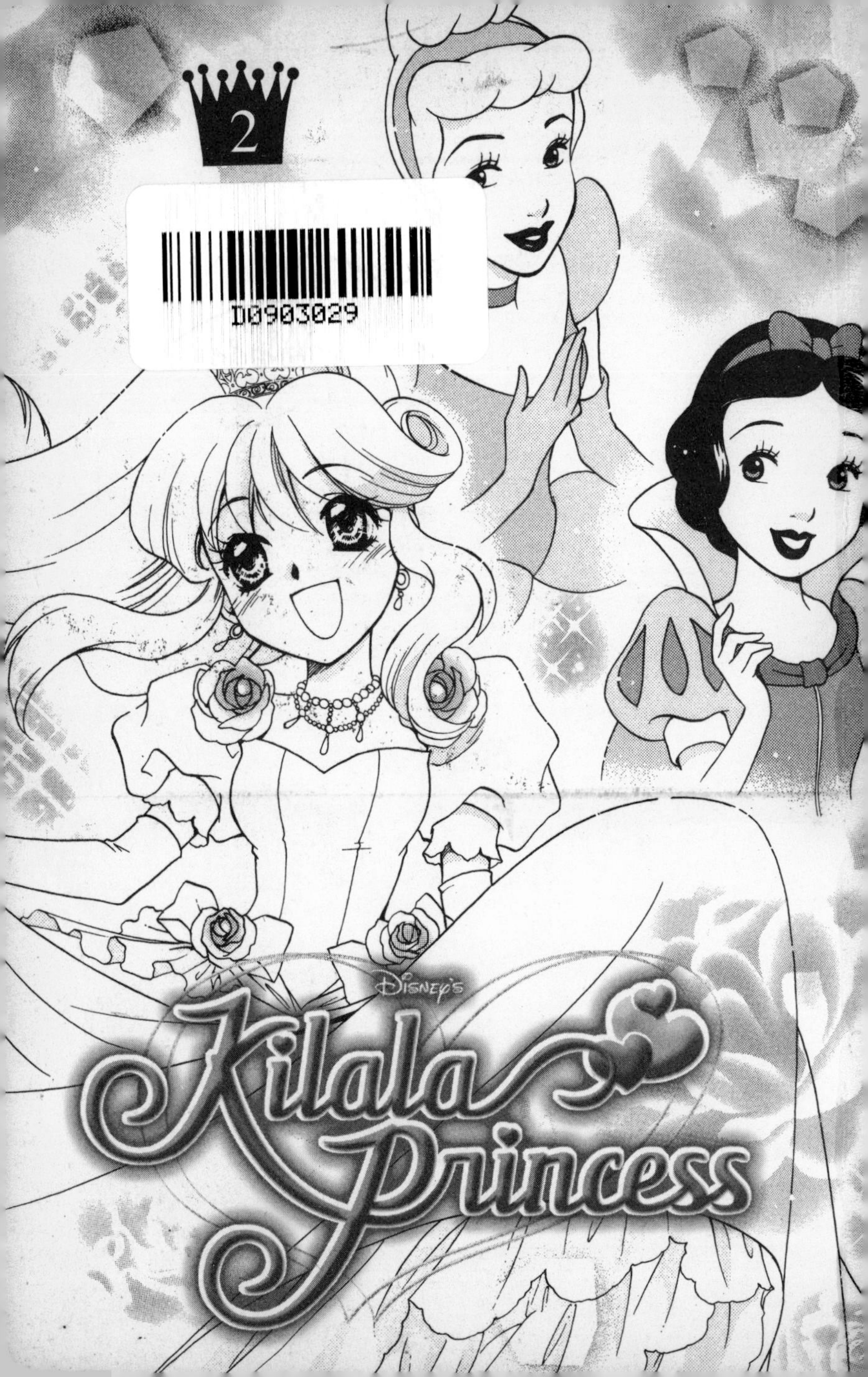
2
Disney's
Kilala Princess

Kilala Princess Volume 2
Written by Rika Tanaka
Illustrated by Nao Kodaka

English Adaptation - Kathy Schilling
Retouch and Lettering - Star Print Brokers
Production Artist - Courtney Geter
Cover Design - Monalisa De Asis

Editor - Hope Donovan
Digital Imaging Manager - Chris Buford
Pre-Production Supervisor - Erika Terriquez
Art Director - Anne Marie Horne
Production Manager - Elisabeth Brizzi
Managing Editor - Vy Nguyen
VP of Production - Ron Klamert
Editor-in-Chief - Rob Tokar
Publisher - Mike Kiley
President and C.O.O. - John Parker
C.E.O. and Chief Creative Officer - Stuart Levy

A  Manga

TOKYOPOP and 🐱 are trademarks or registered trademarks of TOKYOPOP Inc.

TOKYOPOP Inc.
5900 Wilshire Blvd. Suite 2000
Los Angeles, CA 90036

E-mail: info@TOKYOPOP.com
Come visit us online at www.TOKYOPOP.com

ISBN: 978-1-59816-768-9

First TOKYOPOP printing: May 2007
10 9 8 7 6 5 4 3 2 1
Printed in the USA

Disney's

Kilala Princess

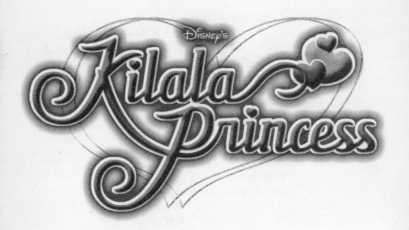

Volume 2

Art by Nao Kodaka
Story by Rika Tanaka

TOKYOPOP®

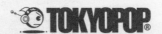

HAMBURG // LONDON // LOS ANGELES // TOKYO

MEET Kilala AND FRIENDS

Kilala
An ordinary girl who loves all the Disney Princesses. Kilala's parents have gone to a faraway land called Paradiso because her mother is sick.

Tippe
Kilala's pet flying mouse.

Kilala's on an adventure to find a princess!

Kilala's best friend Erica was kidnapped! Guided by Rei's tiara, Kilala went through a gate to find her and ended up in the world of Snow White. Now the Evil Queen has captured Kilala and Rei! Who will save the day?

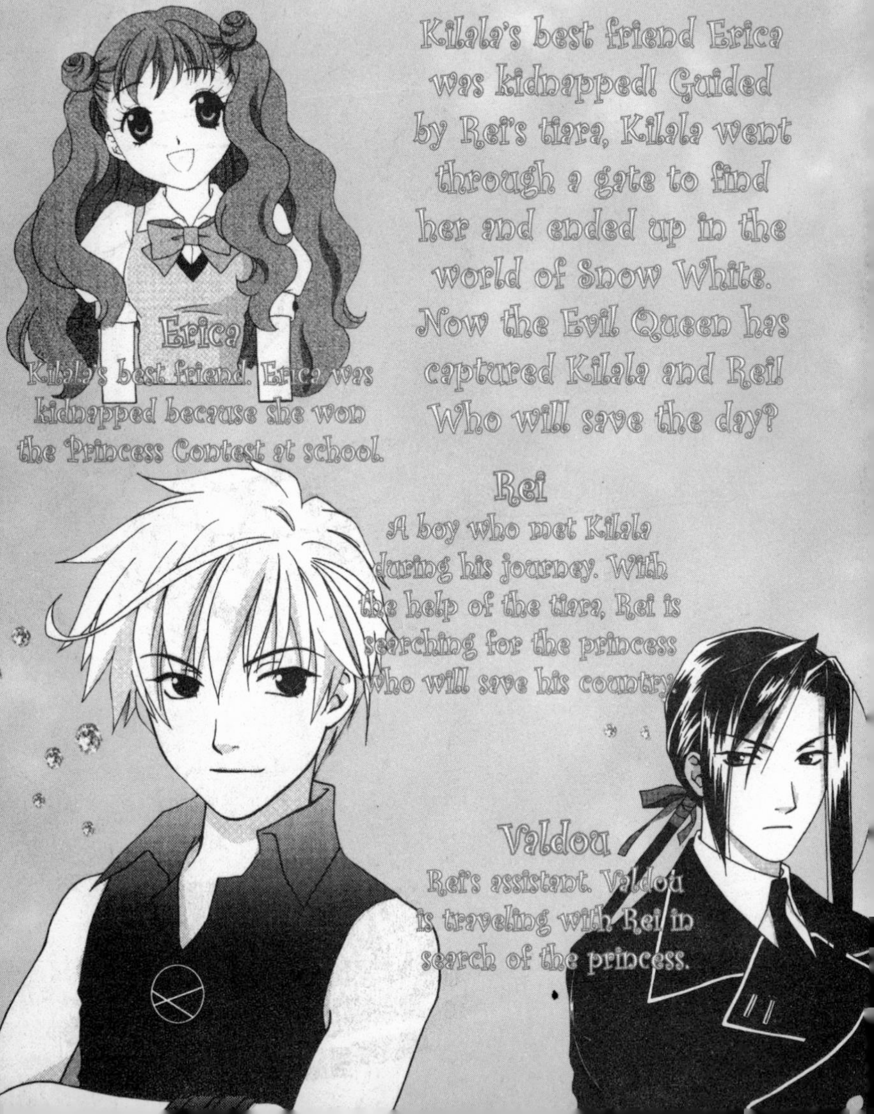

Erica

Kilala's best friend. Erica was kidnapped because she won the Princess Contest at school.

Rei

A boy who met Kilala during his journey. With the help of the tiara, Rei is searching for the princess who will save his country.

Valdou

Rei's assistant. Valdou is traveling with Rei in search of the princess.

Princess
Aurora

Belle

ey
cesses

Ariel

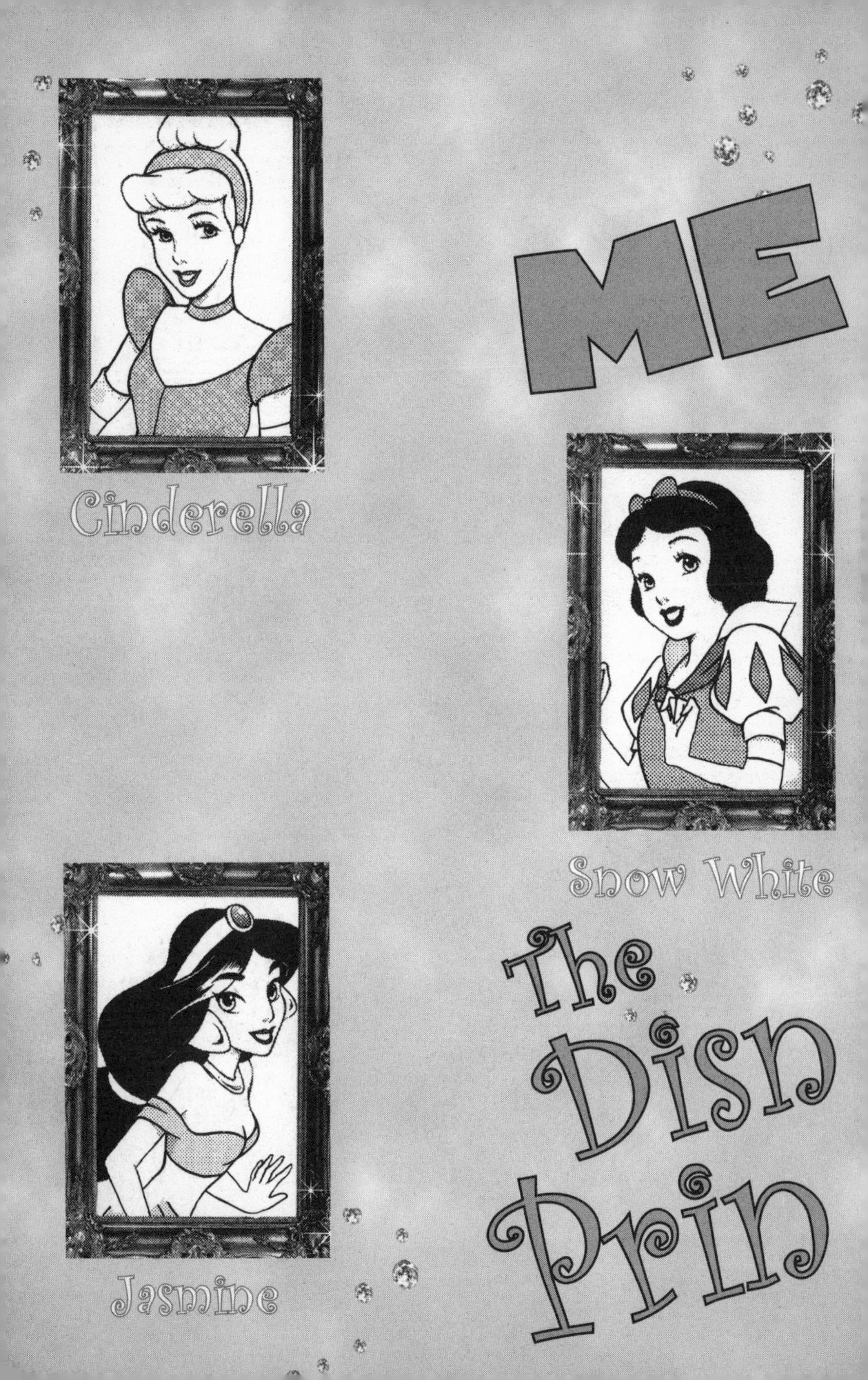
ME
Snow White
The Dish Prin
Cinderella
Jasmine

Contents

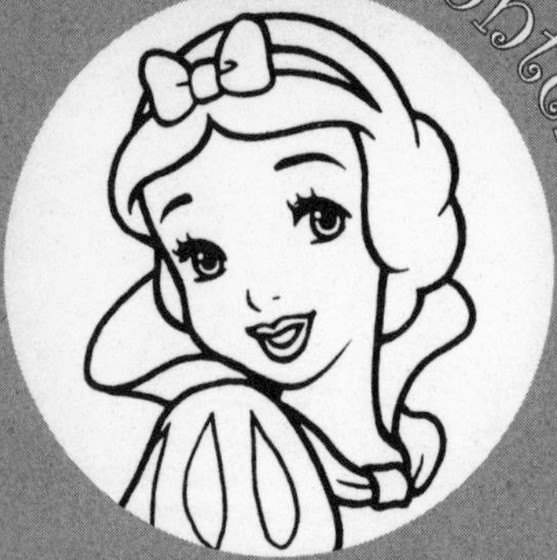

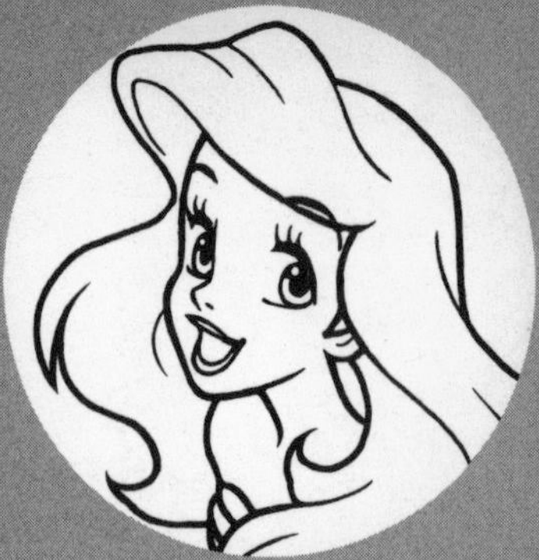

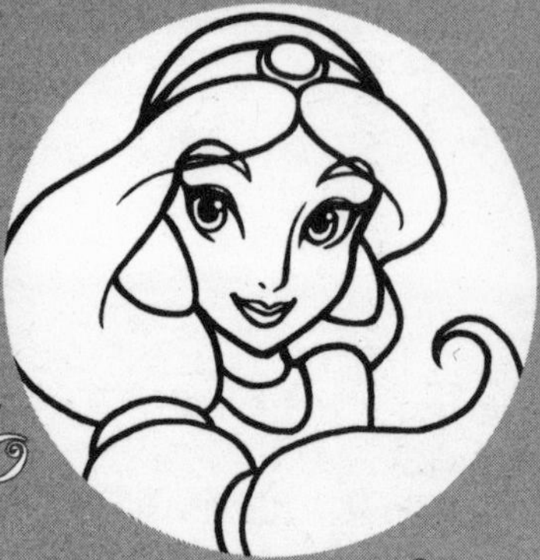

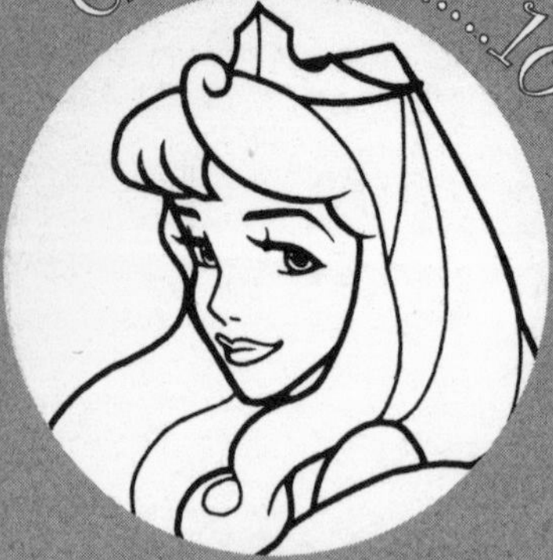

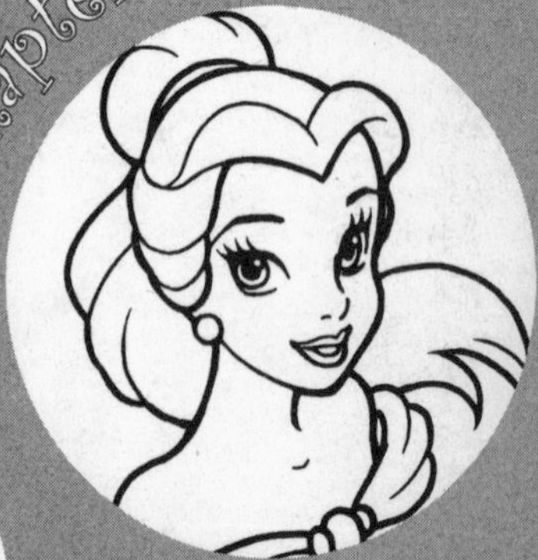

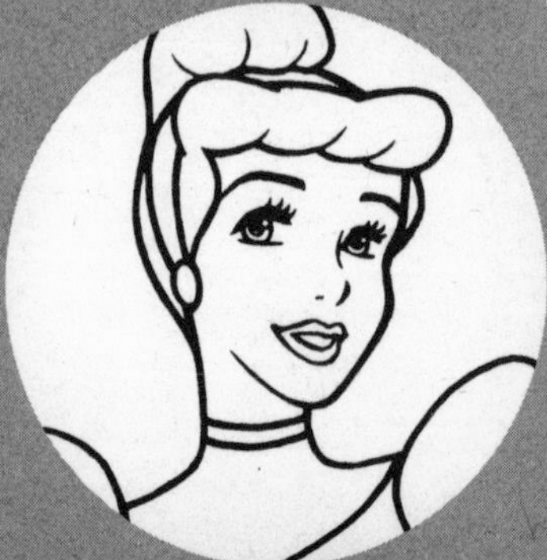

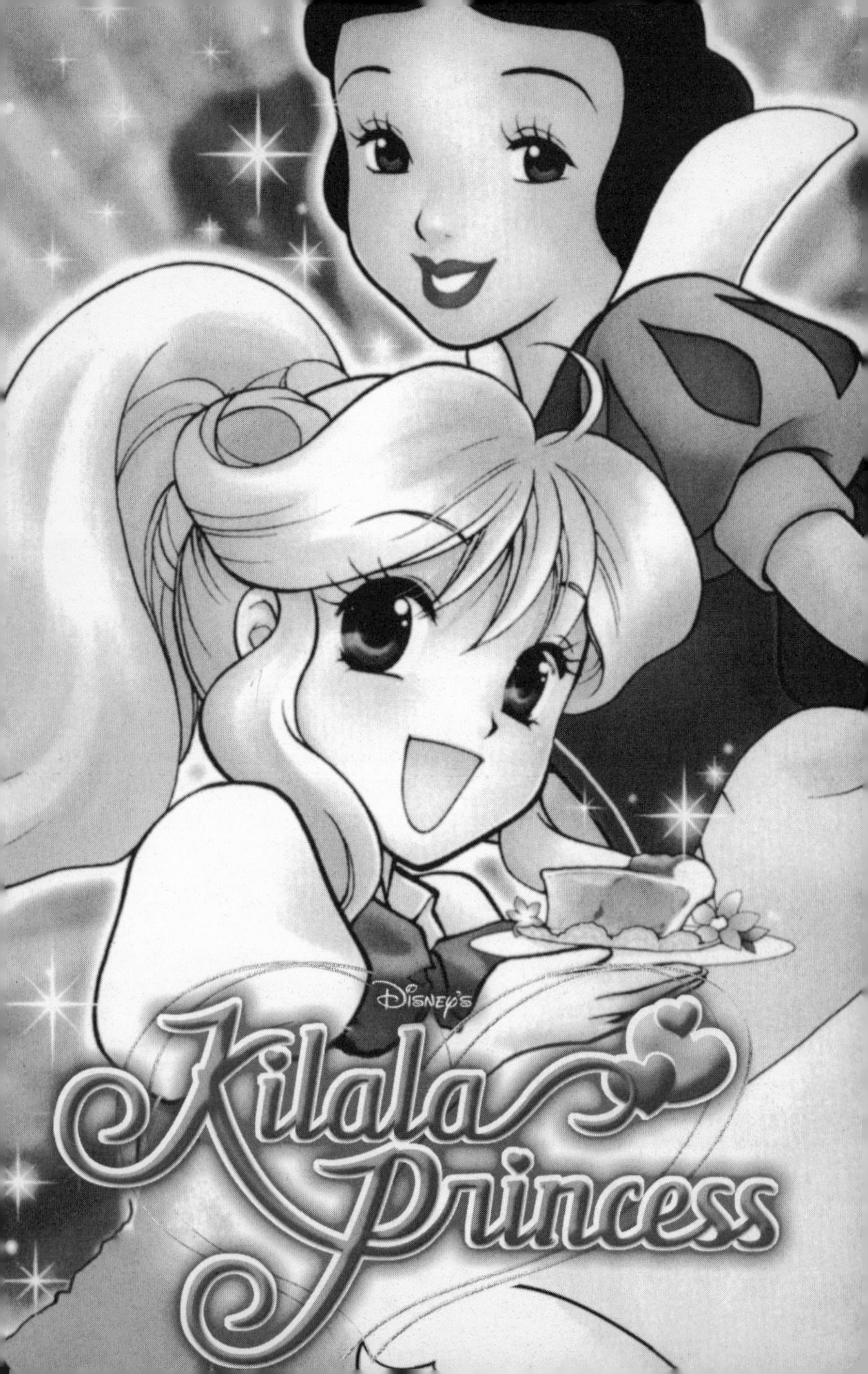
Disney's
Kilala Princess

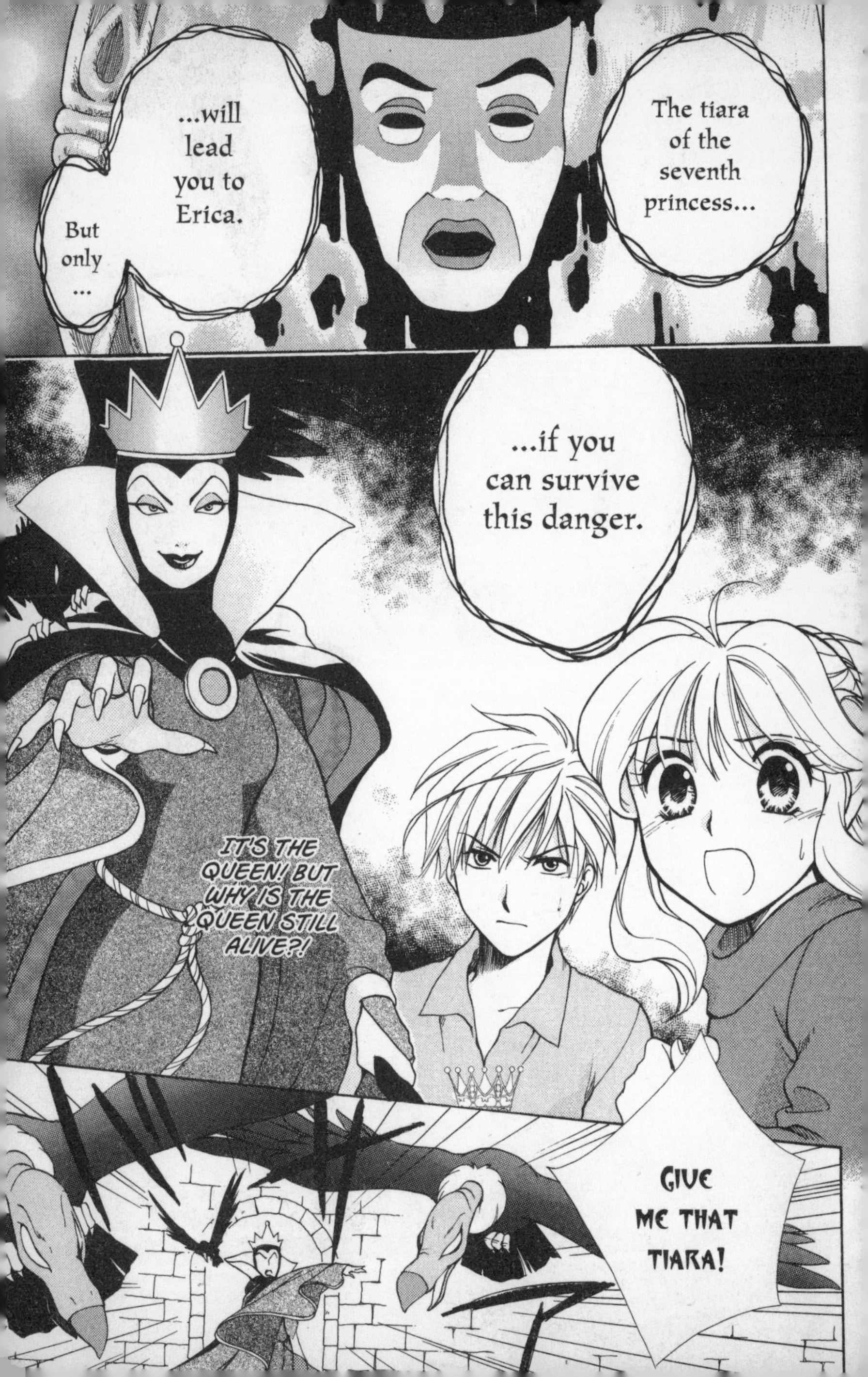
The tiara of the seventh princess...
...will lead you to Erica.
But only ...
...if you can survive this danger.
IT'S THE QUEEN! BUT WHY IS THE QUEEN STILL ALIVE?!
GIVE ME THAT TIARA!

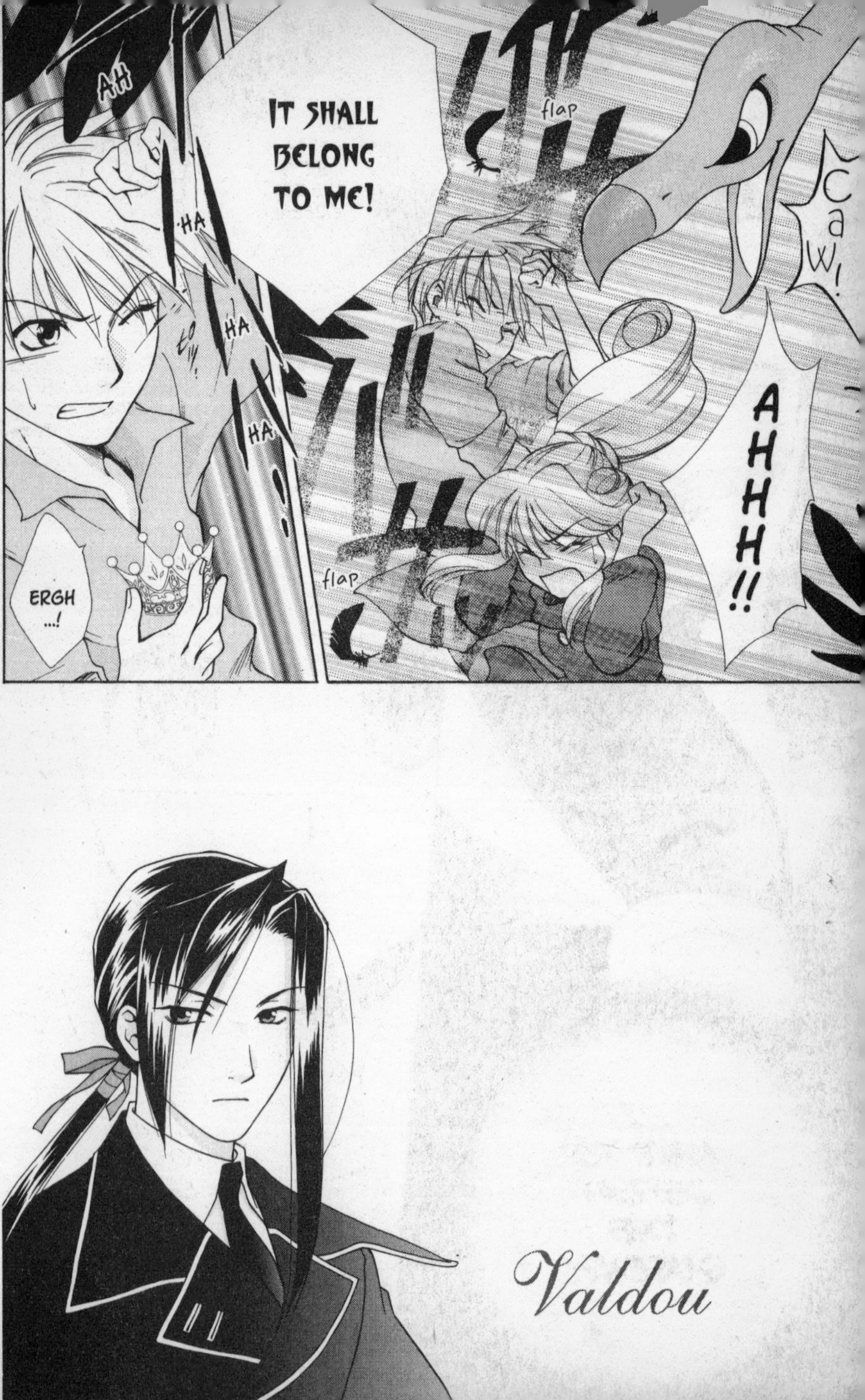
flap
CAW!
AHHH!!
flap
AH
HA
HA
HA
IT SHALL BELONG TO ME!
ERGH ...!
Valdou

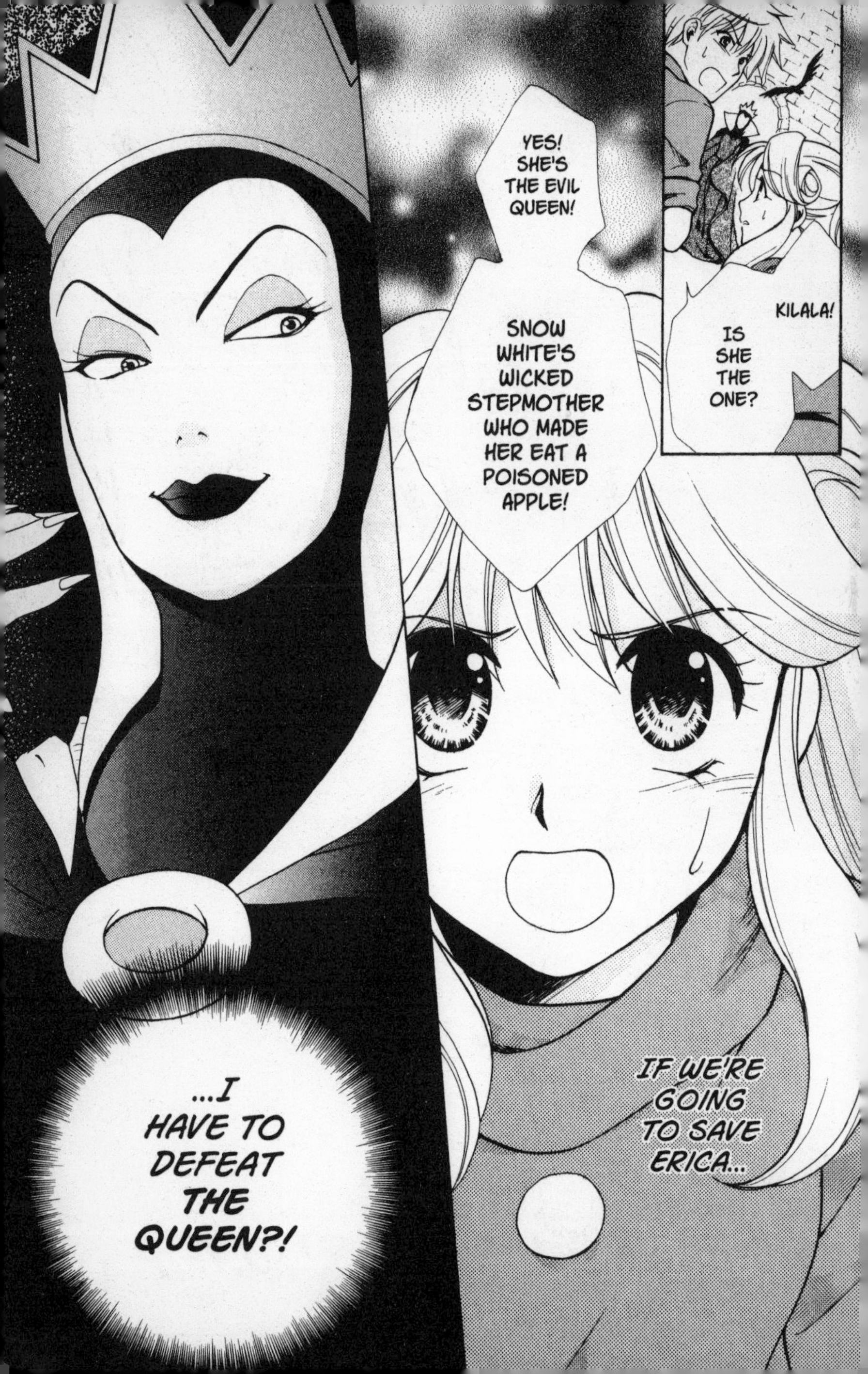
KILALA!
IS SHE THE ONE?
YES! SHE'S THE EVIL QUEEN!
SNOW WHITE'S WICKED STEPMOTHER WHO MADE HER EAT A POISONED APPLE!
IF WE'RE GOING TO SAVE ERICA...
...I HAVE TO DEFEAT THE QUEEN?!

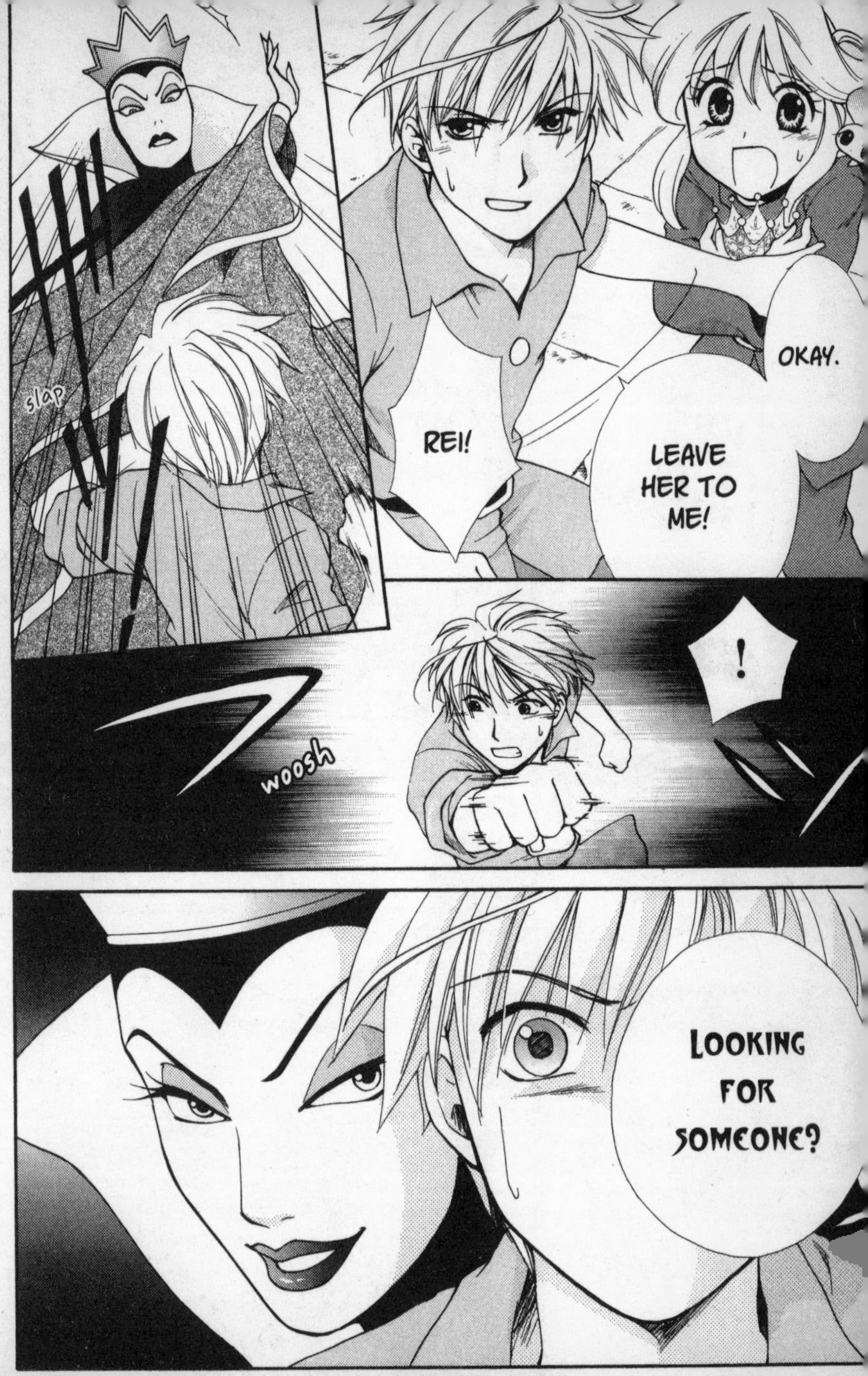
OKAY.
LEAVE HER TO ME!
REI!
slap
!
woosh
LOOKING FOR SOMEONE?

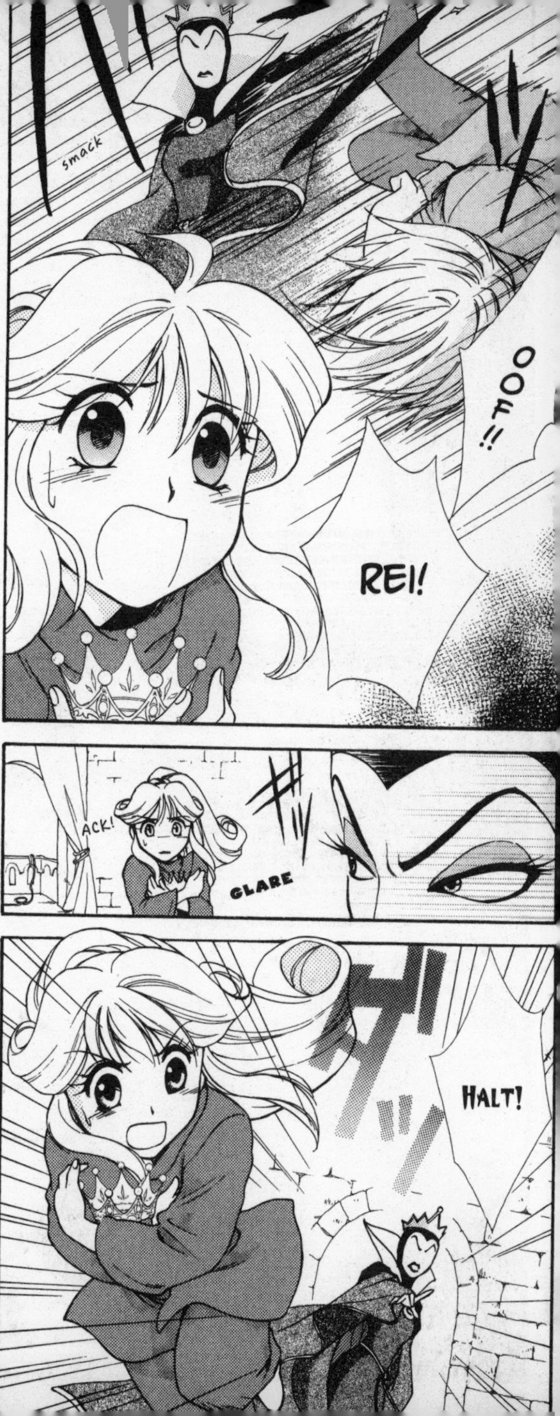
OOF!!
smack
REI!
GLARE
ACK!
HALT!

Snow White

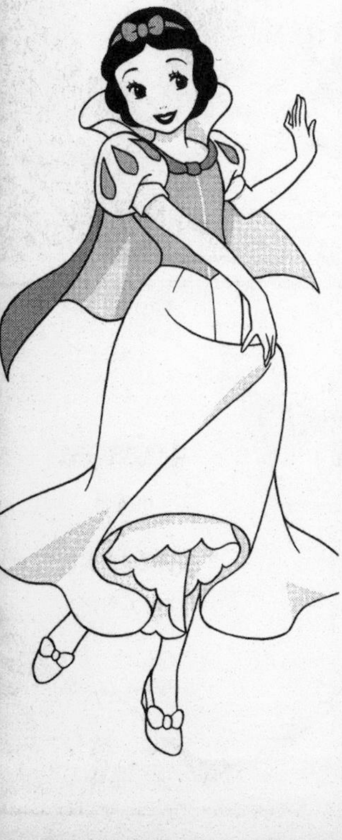

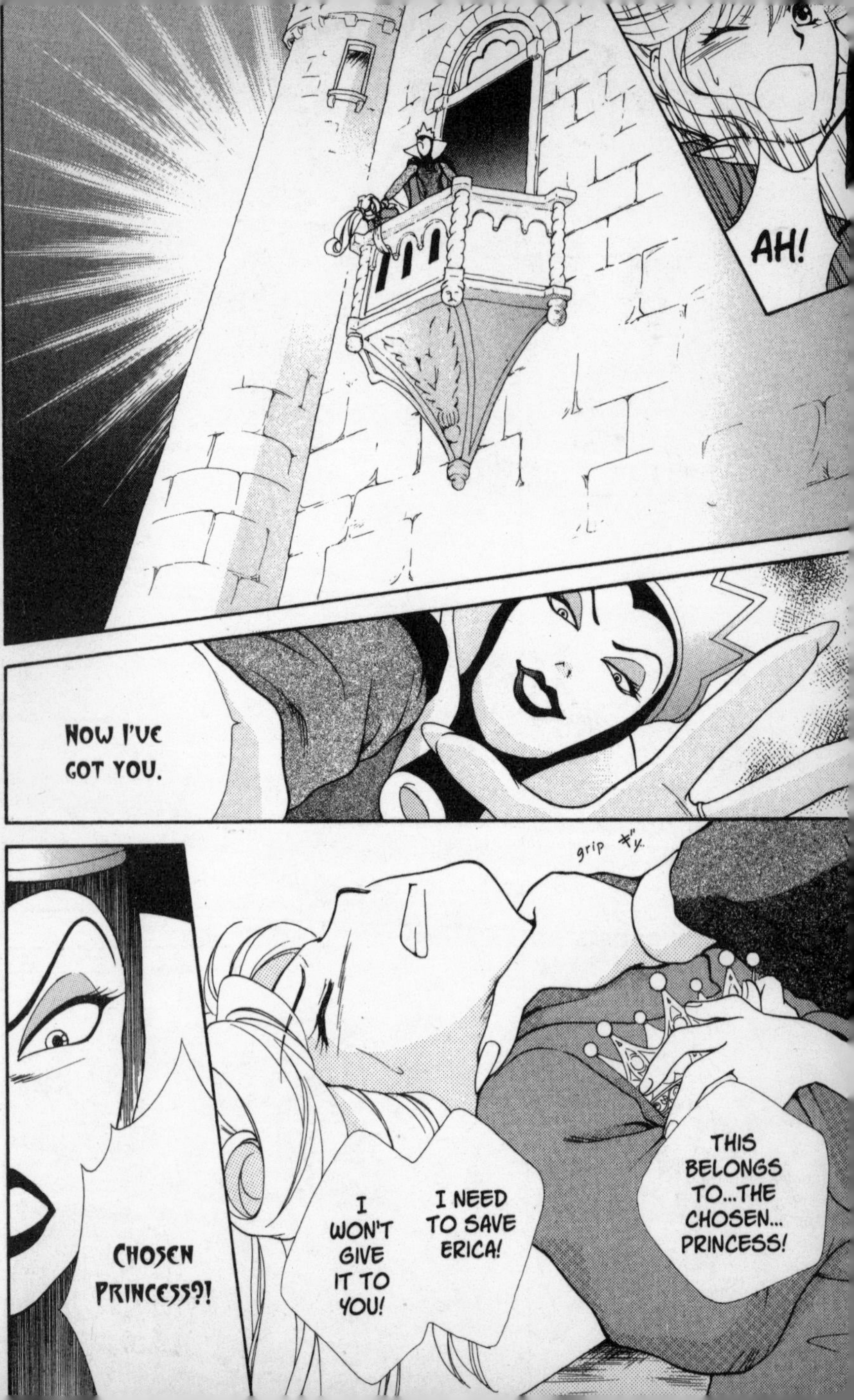
AH!
NOW I'VE GOT YOU.
grip
THIS BELONGS TO...THE CHOSEN... PRINCESS!
I NEED TO SAVE ERICA!
I WON'T GIVE IT TO YOU!
CHOSEN PRINCESS?!

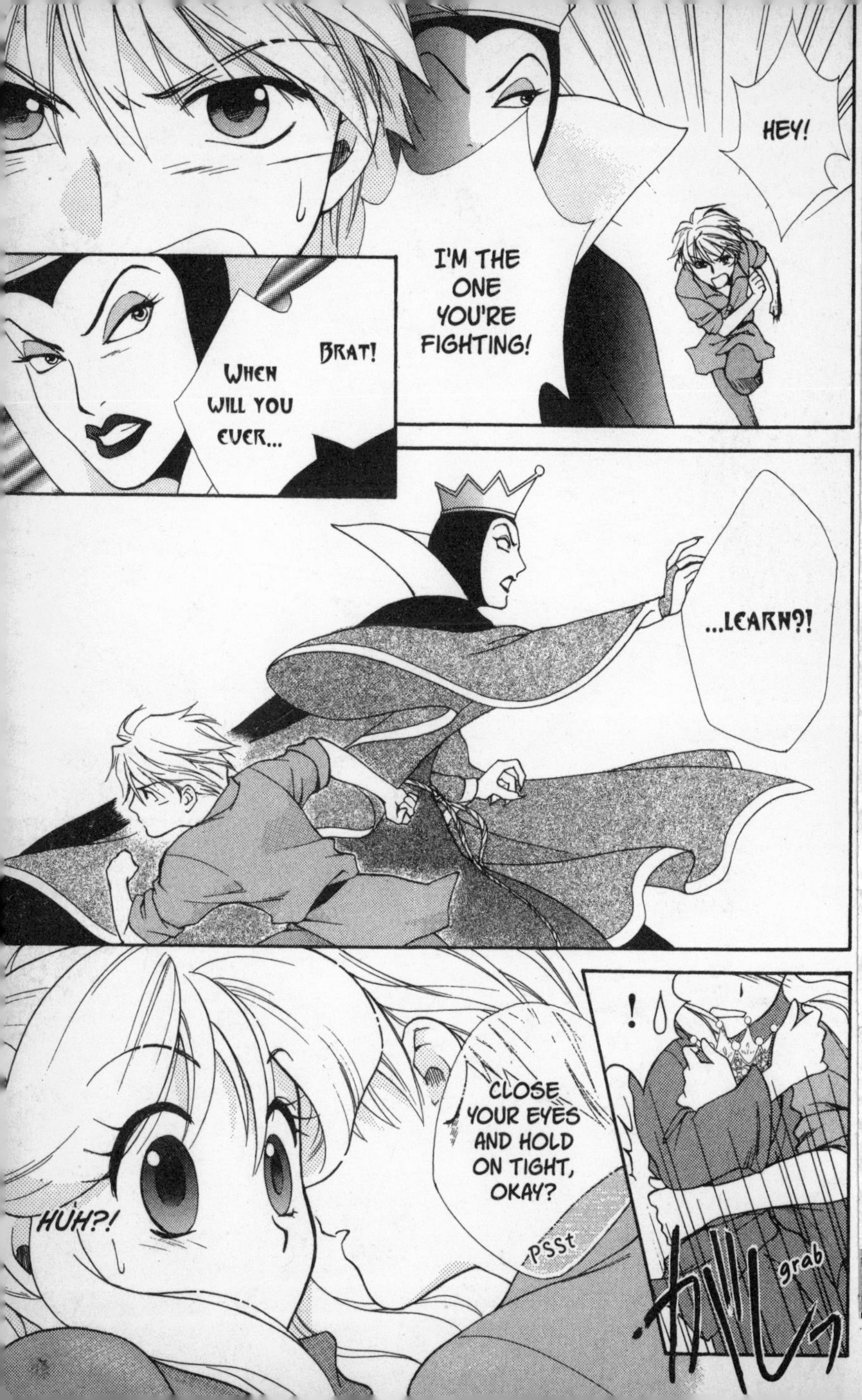
HEY!
I'M THE ONE YOU'RE FIGHTING!
BRAT!
WHEN WILL YOU EVER...
...LEARN?!
!
grab
CLOSE YOUR EYES AND HOLD ON TIGHT, OKAY?
PSSt
HUH?!

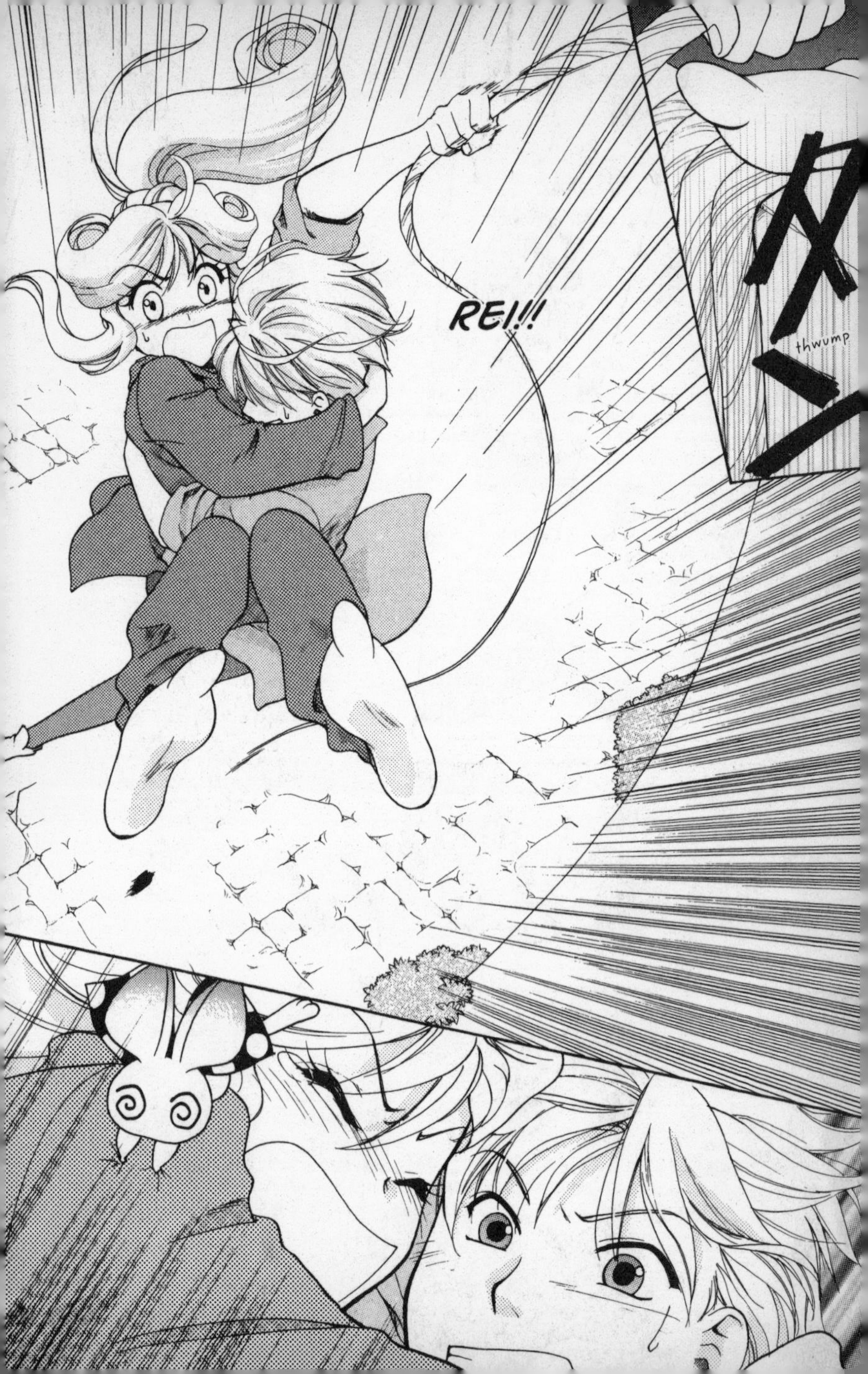
thwump
REI!!

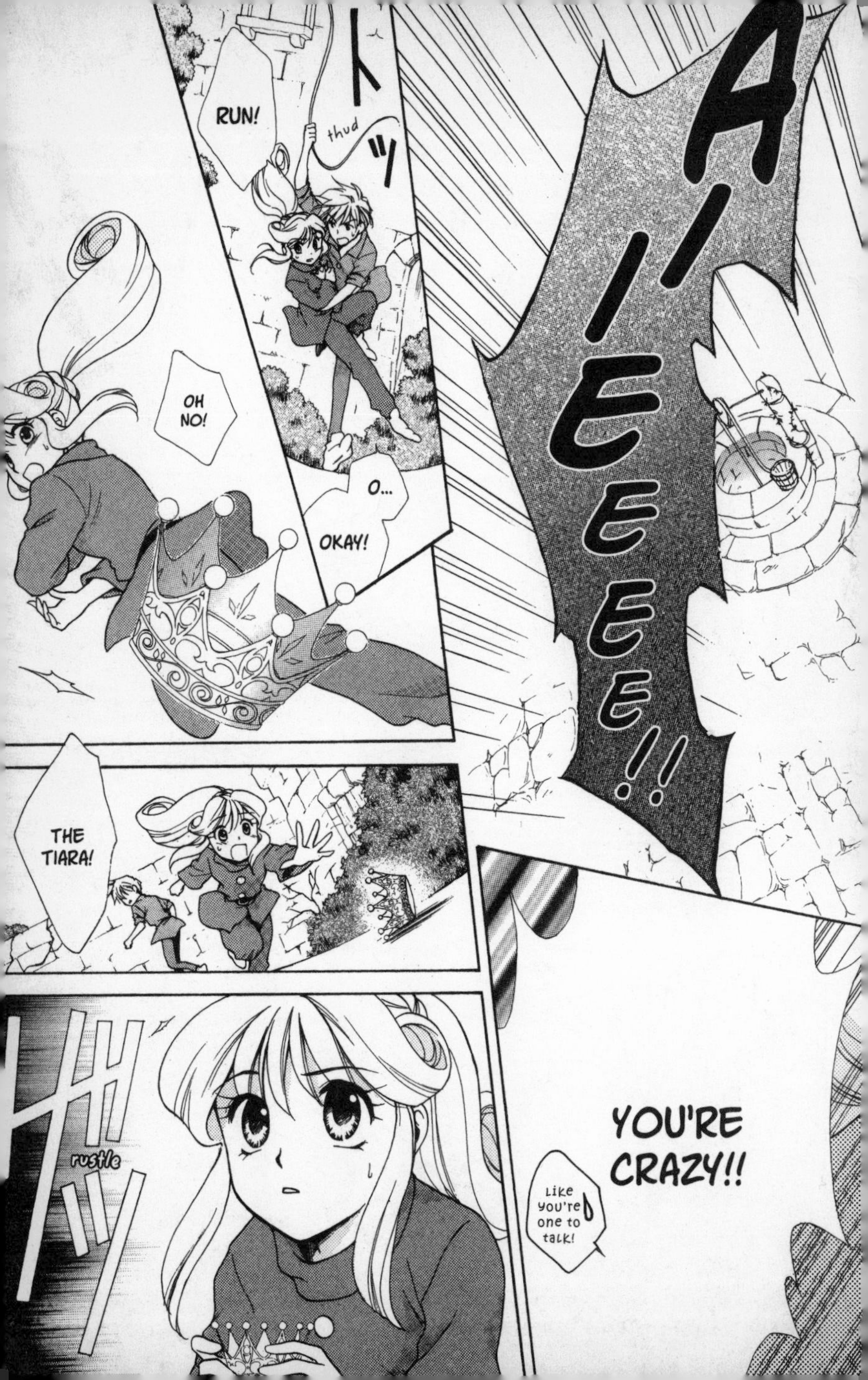
AIIEEEEE!!
RUN!
thud
O... OKAY!
OH NO!
THE TIARA!
YOU'RE CRAZY!!
Like you're one to talk!
rustle

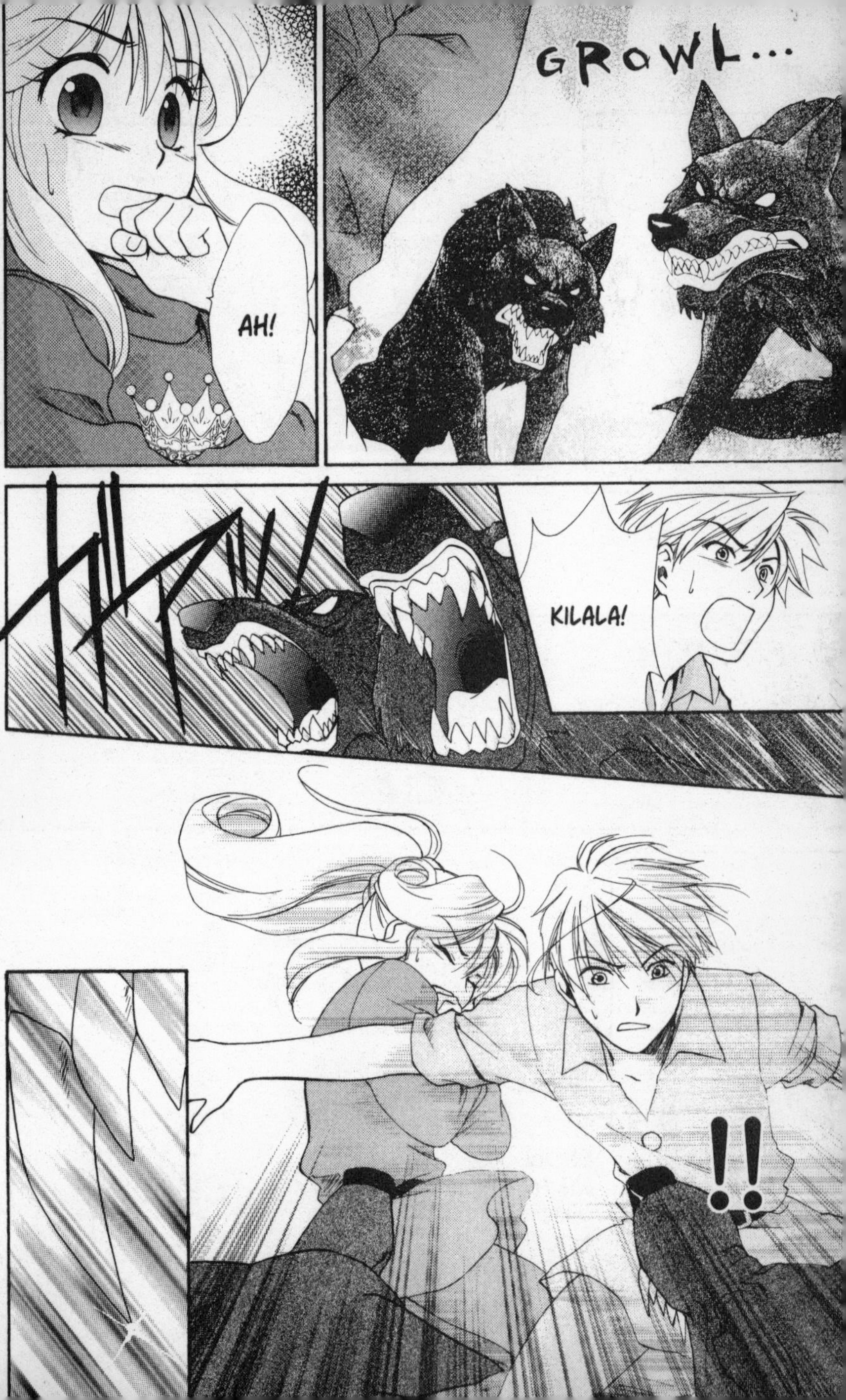
GROWL...
AH!
KILALA!
!!

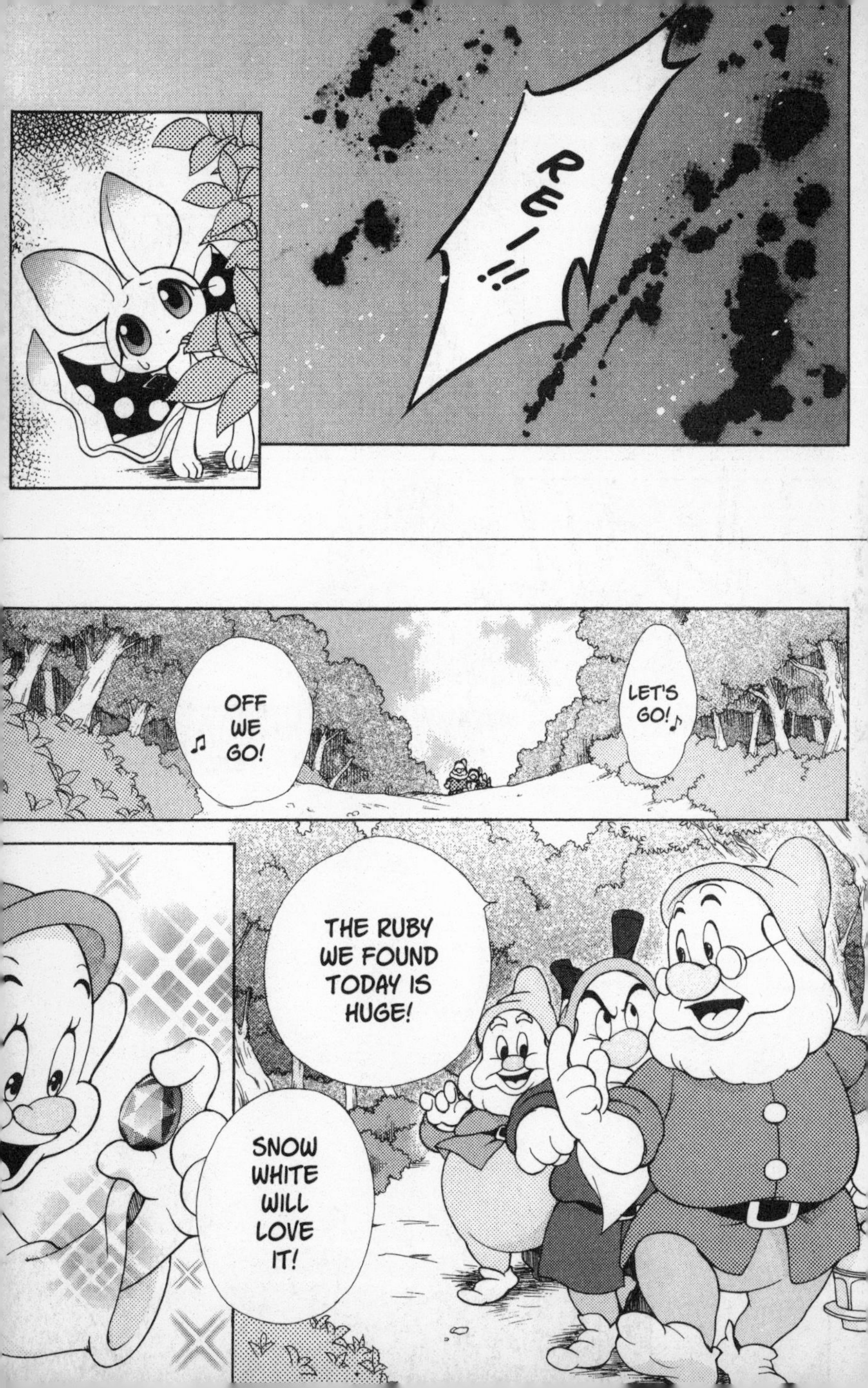
REI—!!
LET'S GO! ♪
OFF WE GO! ♫
THE RUBY WE FOUND TODAY IS HUGE!
SNOW WHITE WILL LOVE IT!

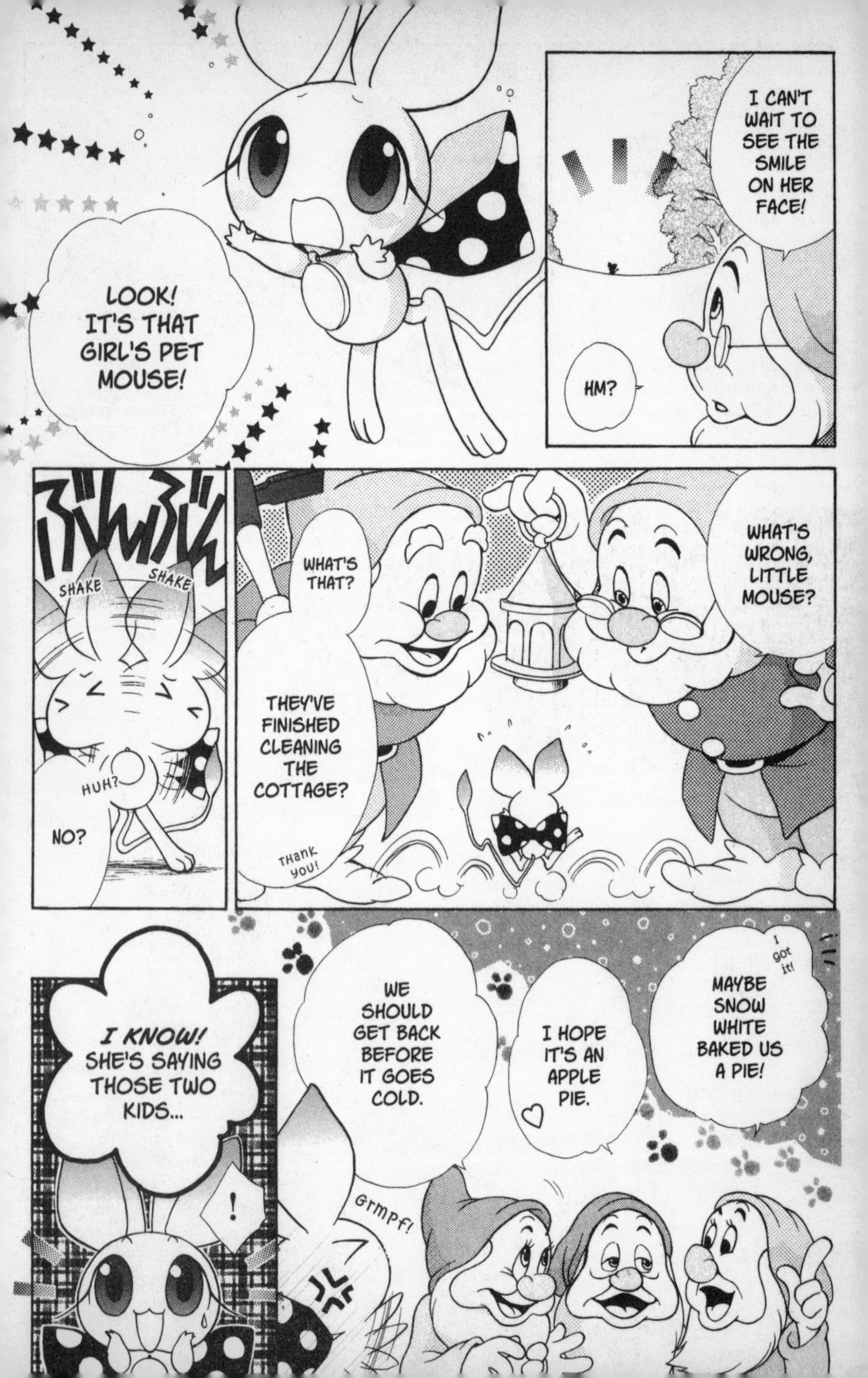
I CAN'T WAIT TO SEE THE SMILE ON HER FACE!
HM?
LOOK! IT'S THAT GIRL'S PET MOUSE!
WHAT'S WRONG, LITTLE MOUSE?
WHAT'S THAT?
THEY'VE FINISHED CLEANING THE COTTAGE?
THANK YOU!
ぶんぶん
SHAKE
SHAKE
HUH?
NO?
I got it!
MAYBE SNOW WHITE BAKED US A PIE!
I HOPE IT'S AN APPLE PIE.
WE SHOULD GET BACK BEFORE IT GOES COLD.
Grmpf!
I KNOW! SHE'S SAYING THOSE TWO KIDS...
!

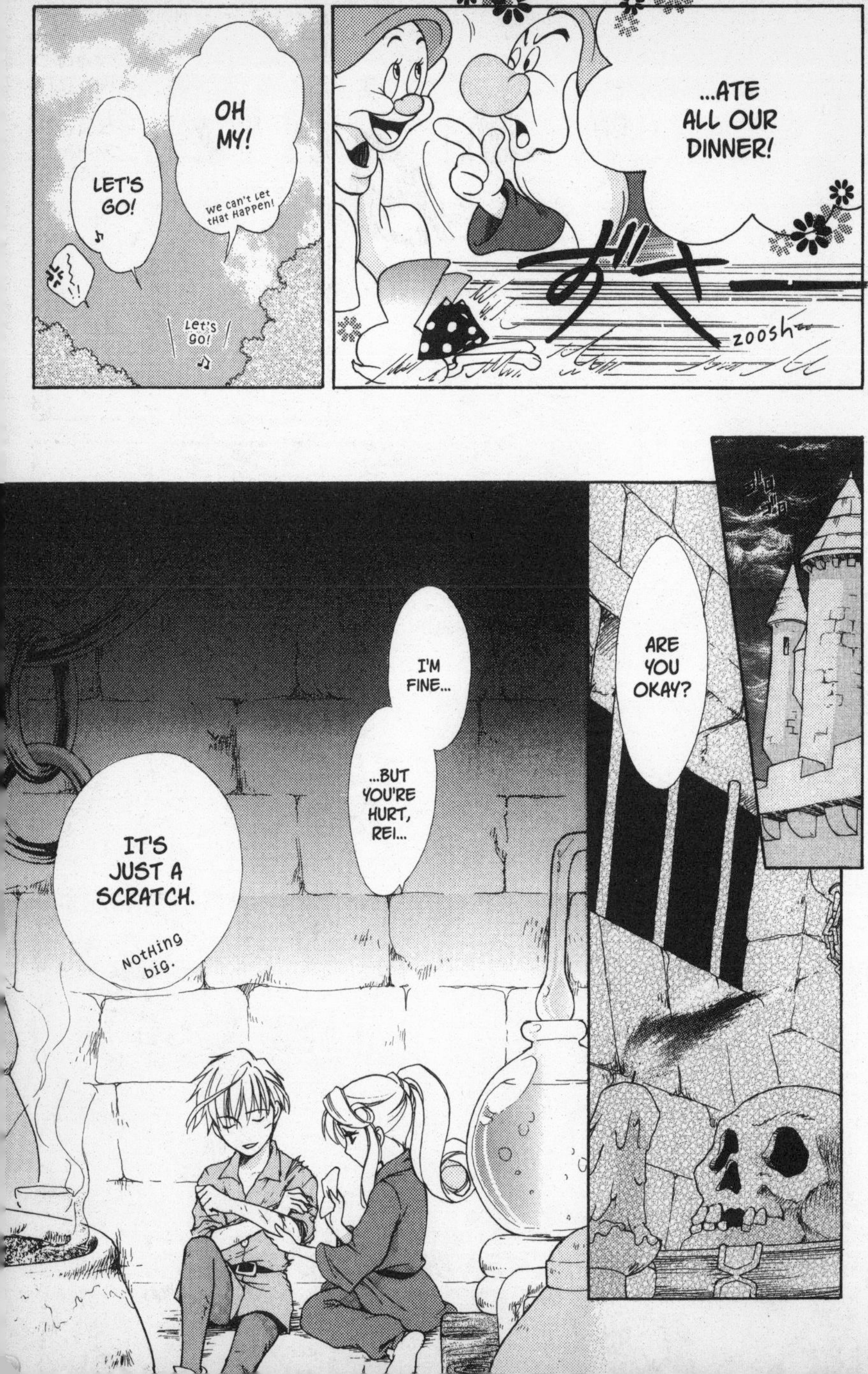
...ATE ALL OUR DINNER!
zoosh
OH MY!
We can't let that Happen!
LET'S GO!
Let's go!
ARE YOU OKAY?
I'M FINE...
...BUT YOU'RE HURT, REI...
IT'S JUST A SCRATCH.
Nothing big.

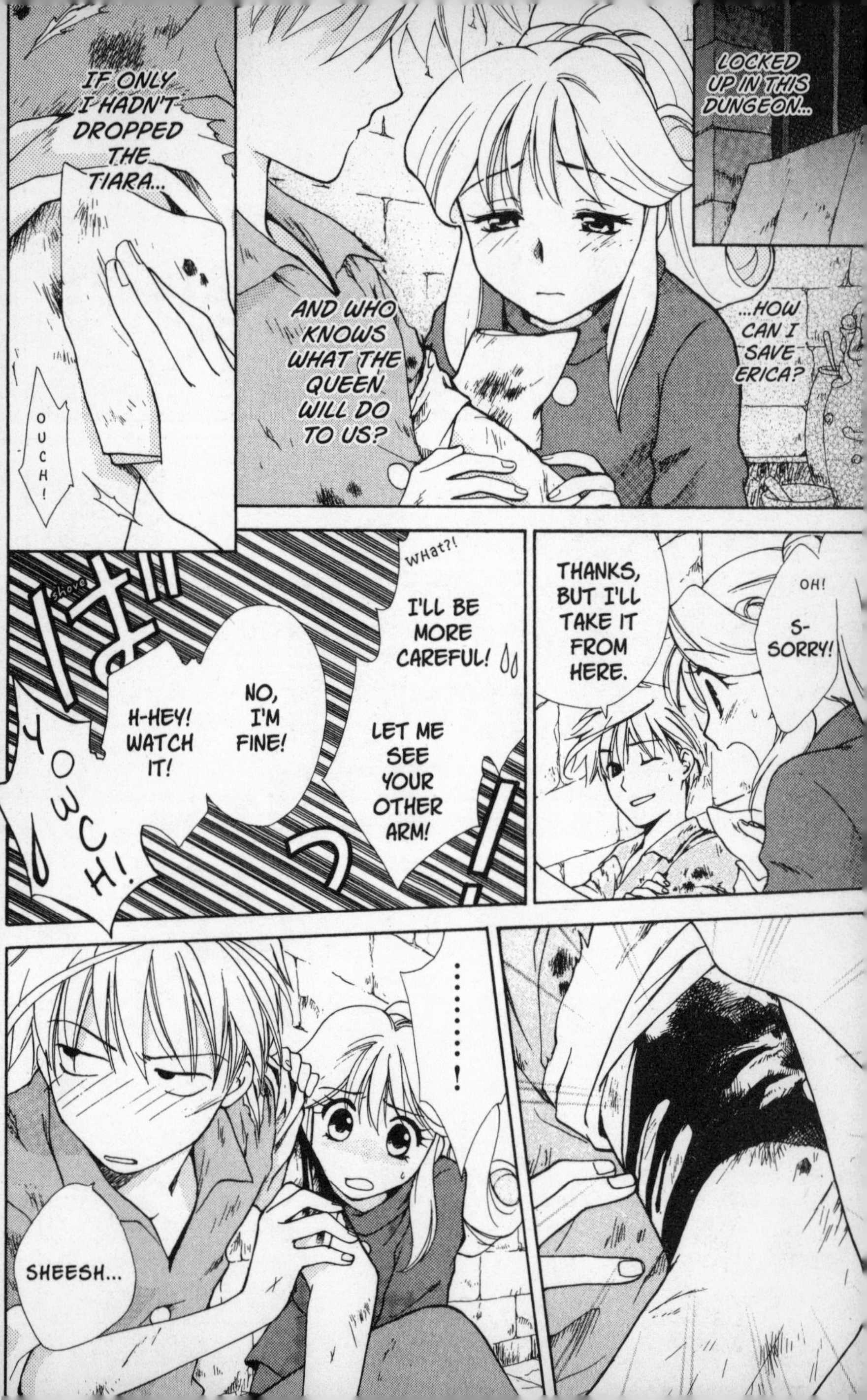
LOCKED UP IN THIS DUNGEON...
...HOW CAN I SAVE ERICA?
AND WHO KNOWS WHAT THE QUEEN WILL DO TO US?
IF ONLY I HADN'T DROPPED THE TIARA...
OUCH!
OH!
S-SORRY!
THANKS, BUT I'LL TAKE IT FROM HERE.
WHAT?!
I'LL BE MORE CAREFUL!
LET ME SEE YOUR OTHER ARM!
NO, I'M FINE!
shove
H-HEY! WATCH IT!
YOWCH!
......!
SHEESH...

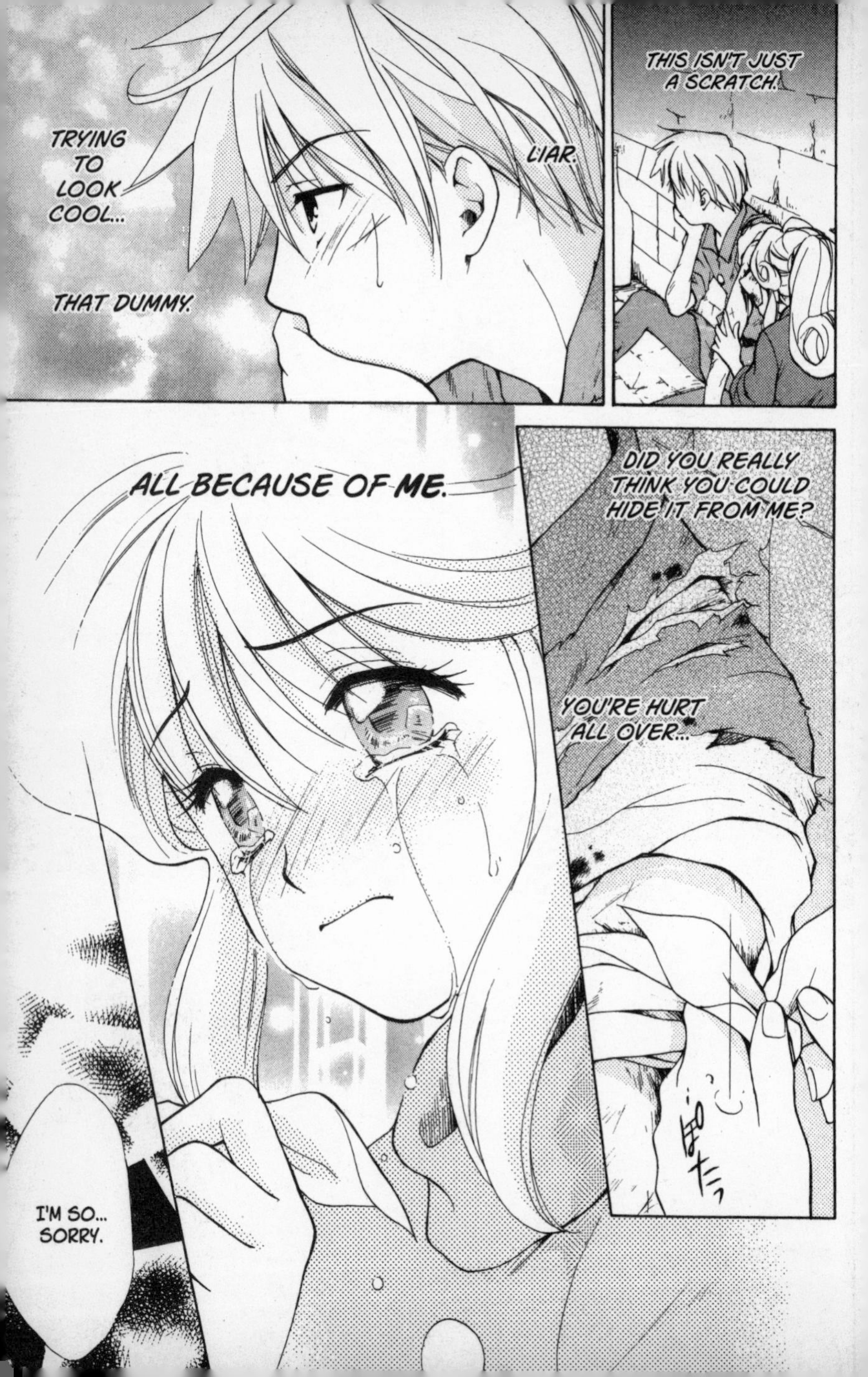
THIS ISN'T JUST A SCRATCH.
LIAR.
TRYING TO LOOK COOL...
THAT DUMMY.
DID YOU REALLY THINK YOU COULD HIDE IT FROM ME?
YOU'RE HURT ALL OVER...
ぽたっ
ALL BECAUSE OF ME.
I'M SO... SORRY.

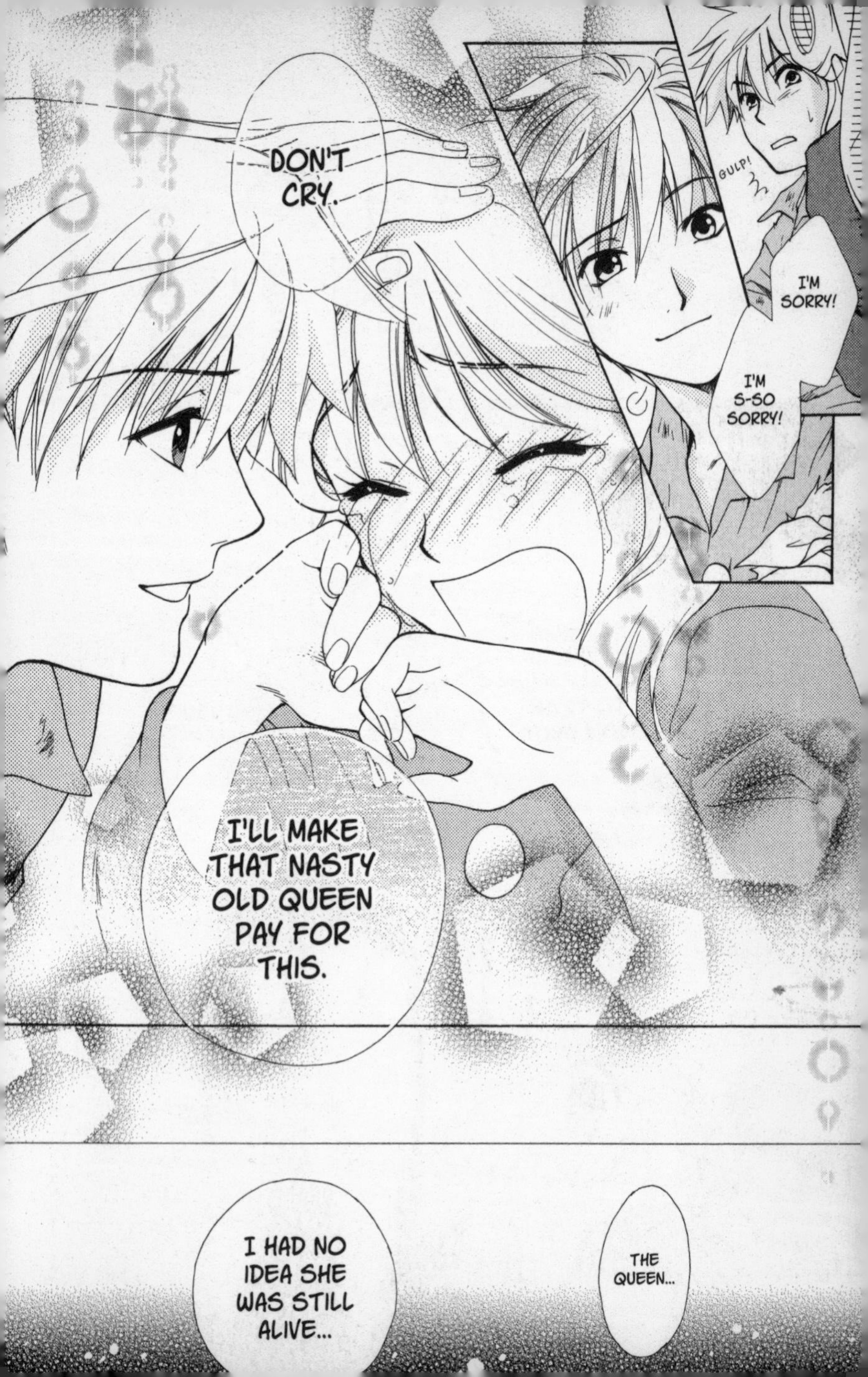
GULP!
I'M SORRY!
I'M S-SO SORRY!
DON'T CRY.
I'LL MAKE THAT NASTY OLD QUEEN PAY FOR THIS.
THE QUEEN...
I HAD NO IDEA SHE WAS STILL ALIVE...

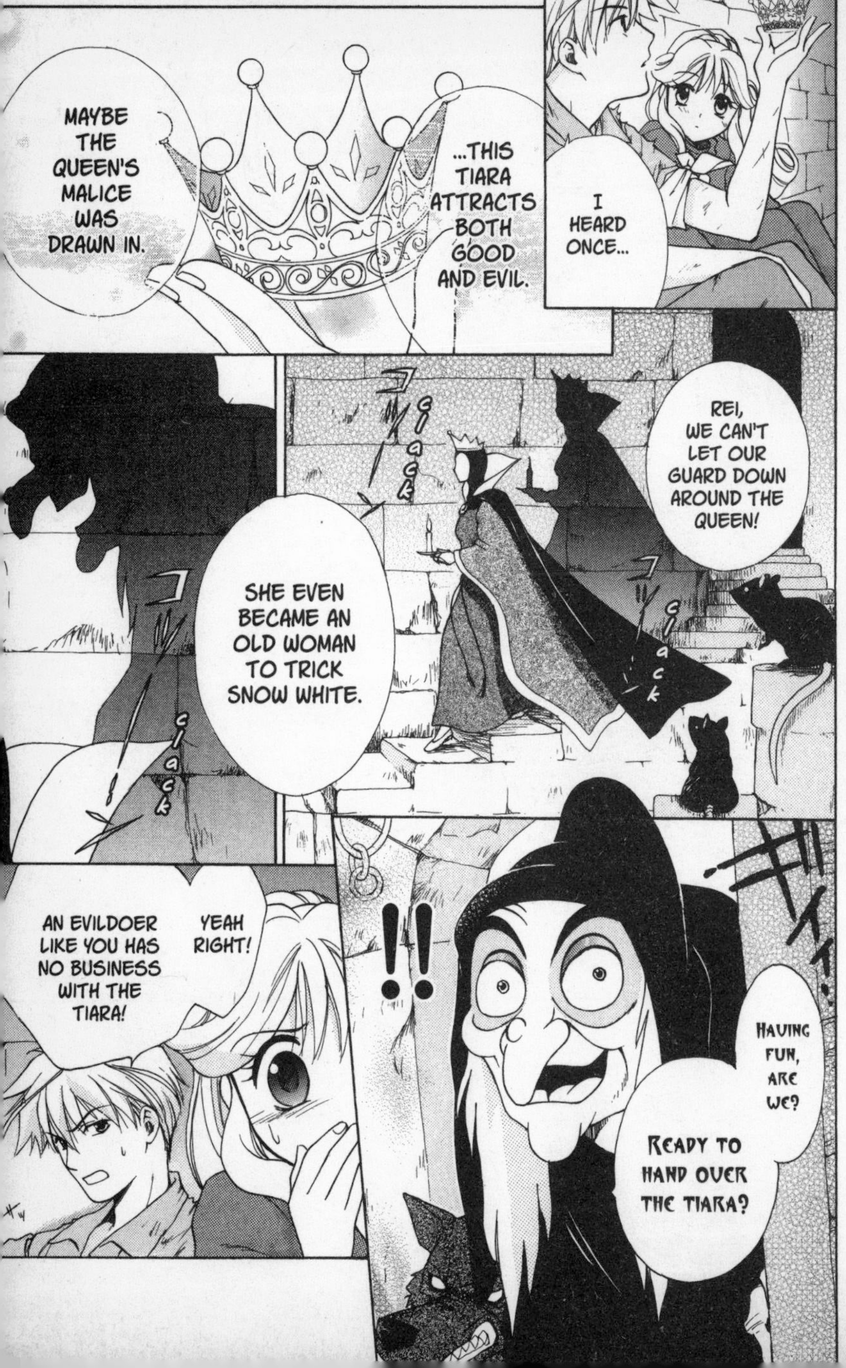
I HEARD ONCE...
...THIS TIARA ATTRACTS BOTH GOOD AND EVIL.
MAYBE THE QUEEN'S MALICE WAS DRAWN IN.
REI, WE CAN'T LET OUR GUARD DOWN AROUND THE QUEEN!
clack
clack
SHE EVEN BECAME AN OLD WOMAN TO TRICK SNOW WHITE.
clack
HAVING FUN, ARE WE?
READY TO HAND OVER THE TIARA?
!!
YEAH RIGHT!
AN EVILDOER LIKE YOU HAS NO BUSINESS WITH THE TIARA!

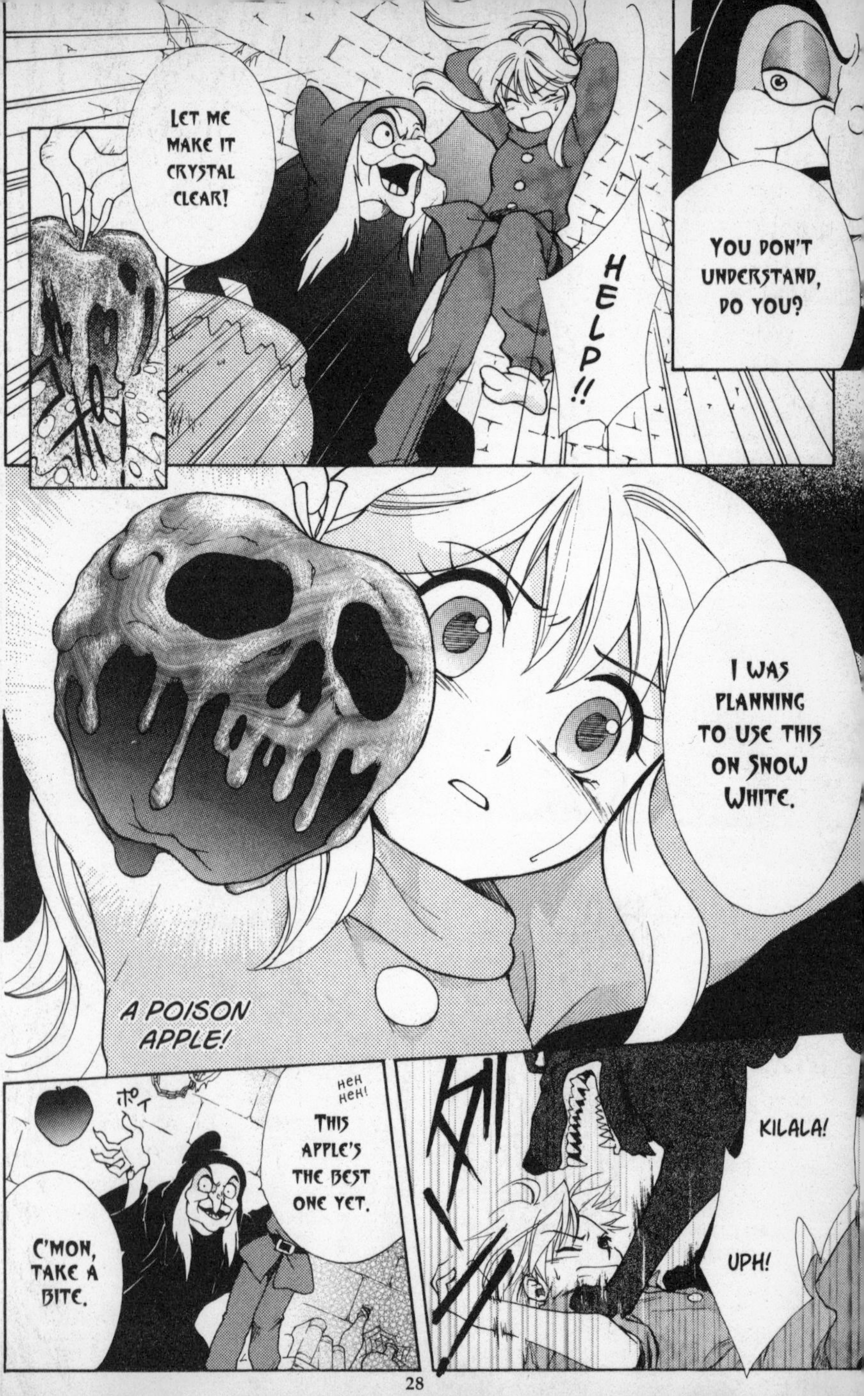
YOU DON'T UNDERSTAND, DO YOU?
LET ME MAKE IT CRYSTAL CLEAR!
HELP!!
I WAS PLANNING TO USE THIS ON SNOW WHITE.
A POISON APPLE!
KILALA!
UPH!
HEH HEH!
THIS APPLE'S THE BEST ONE YET.
C'MON, TAKE A BITE.

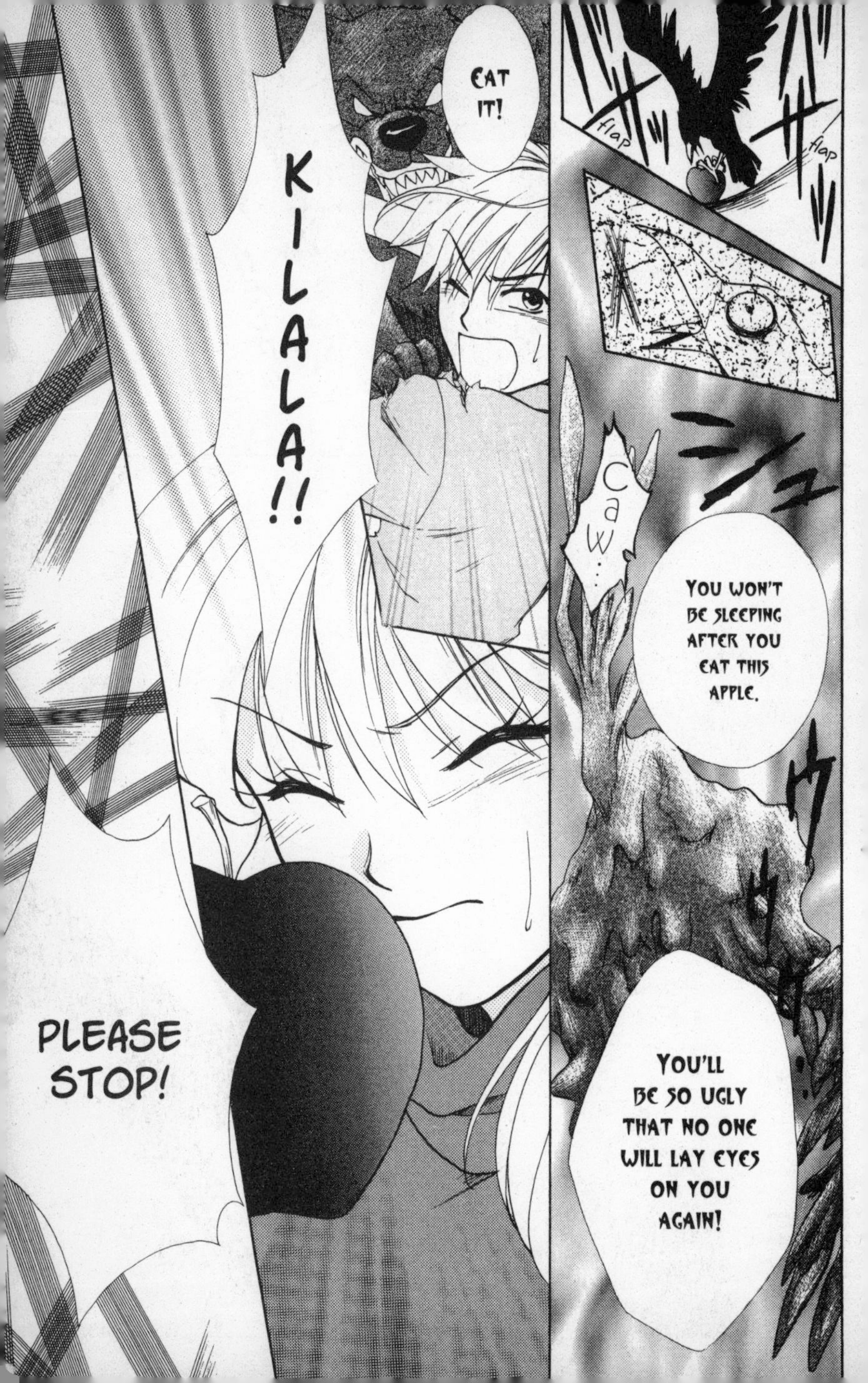
flap
flap
Caw...
YOU WON'T BE SLEEPING AFTER YOU EAT THIS APPLE.
YOU'LL BE SO UGLY THAT NO ONE WILL LAY EYES ON YOU AGAIN!
EAT IT!
KILLALA!!
PLEASE STOP!

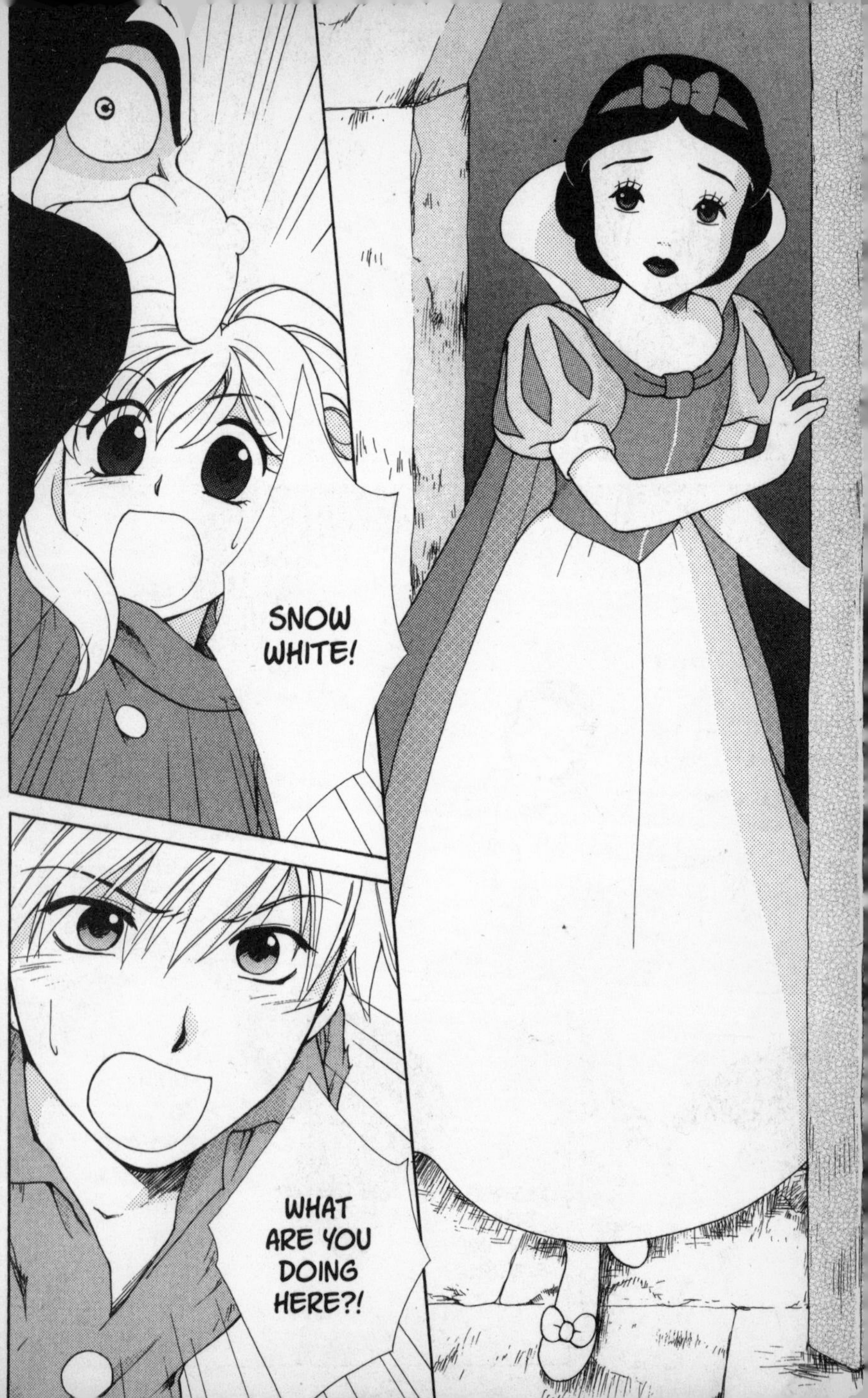
SNOW WHITE!
WHAT ARE YOU DOING HERE?!

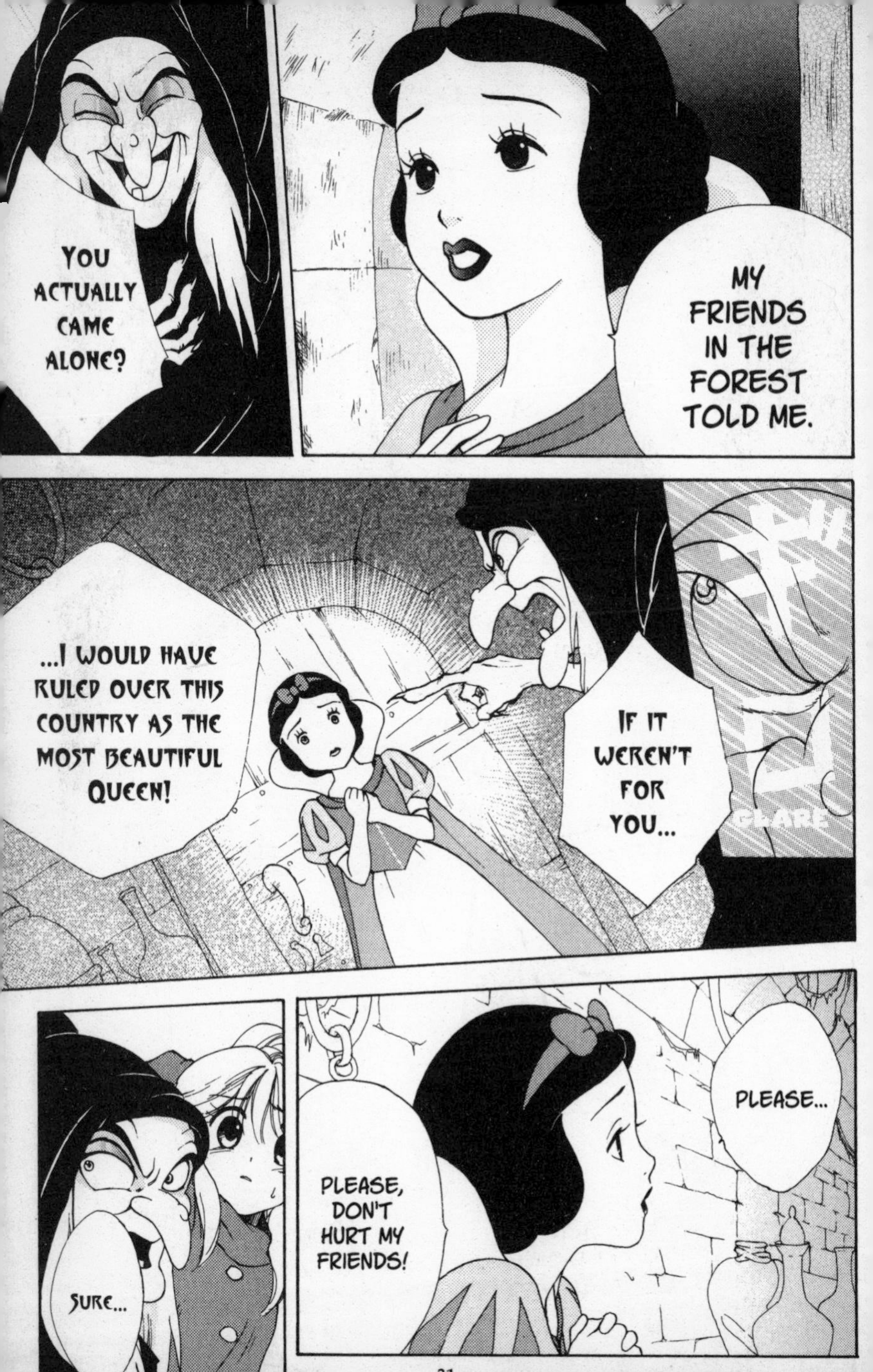
MY FRIENDS IN THE FOREST TOLD ME.
YOU ACTUALLY CAME ALONE?
GLARE
IF IT WEREN'T FOR YOU...
...I WOULD HAVE RULED OVER THIS COUNTRY AS THE MOST BEAUTIFUL QUEEN!
PLEASE...
PLEASE, DON'T HURT MY FRIENDS!
SURE...

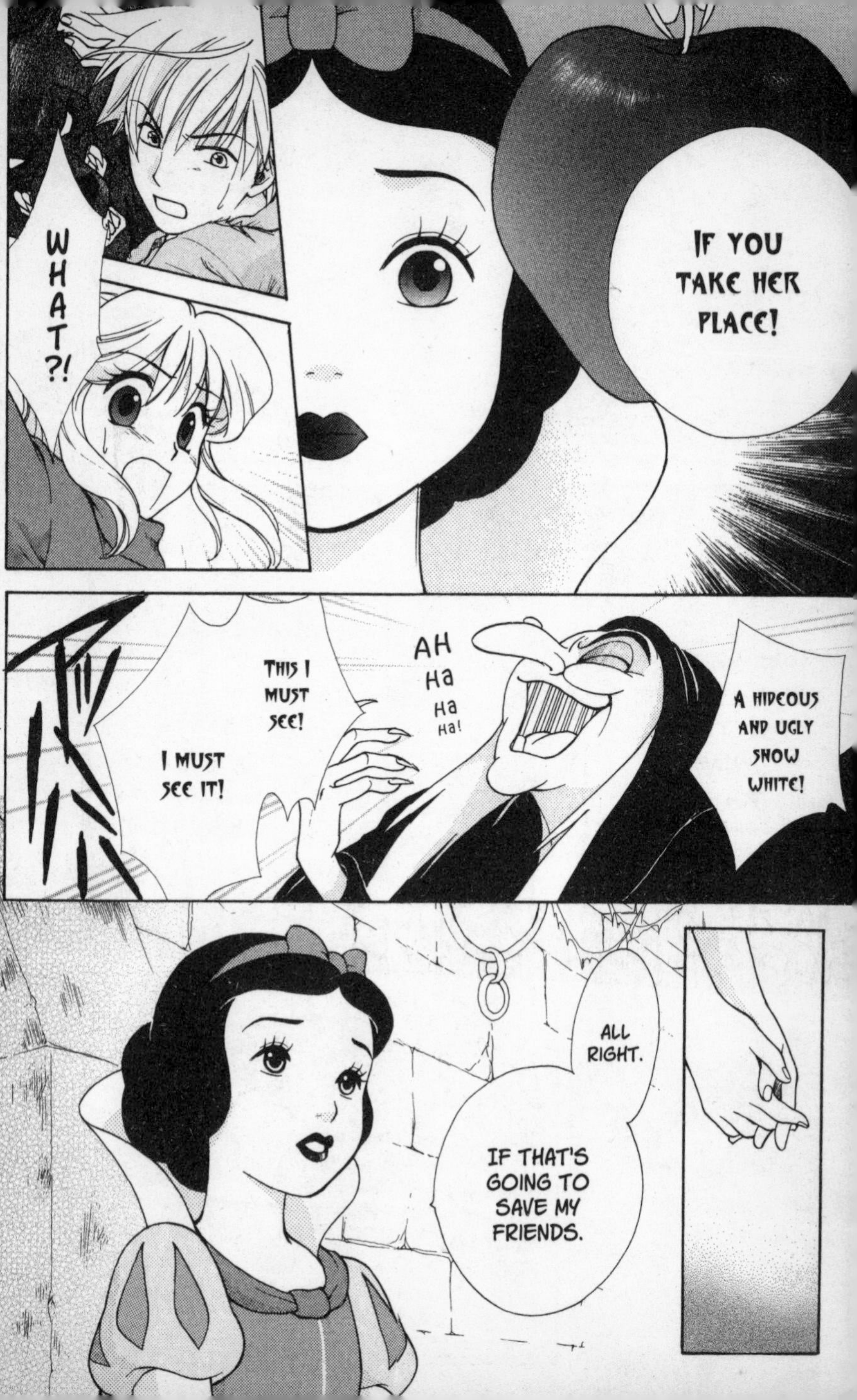
IF YOU TAKE HER PLACE!
WHAT?!
A HIDEOUS AND UGLY SNOW WHITE!
AH Ha Ha Ha!
THIS I MUST SEE!
I MUST SEE IT!
ALL RIGHT.
IF THAT'S GOING TO SAVE MY FRIENDS.

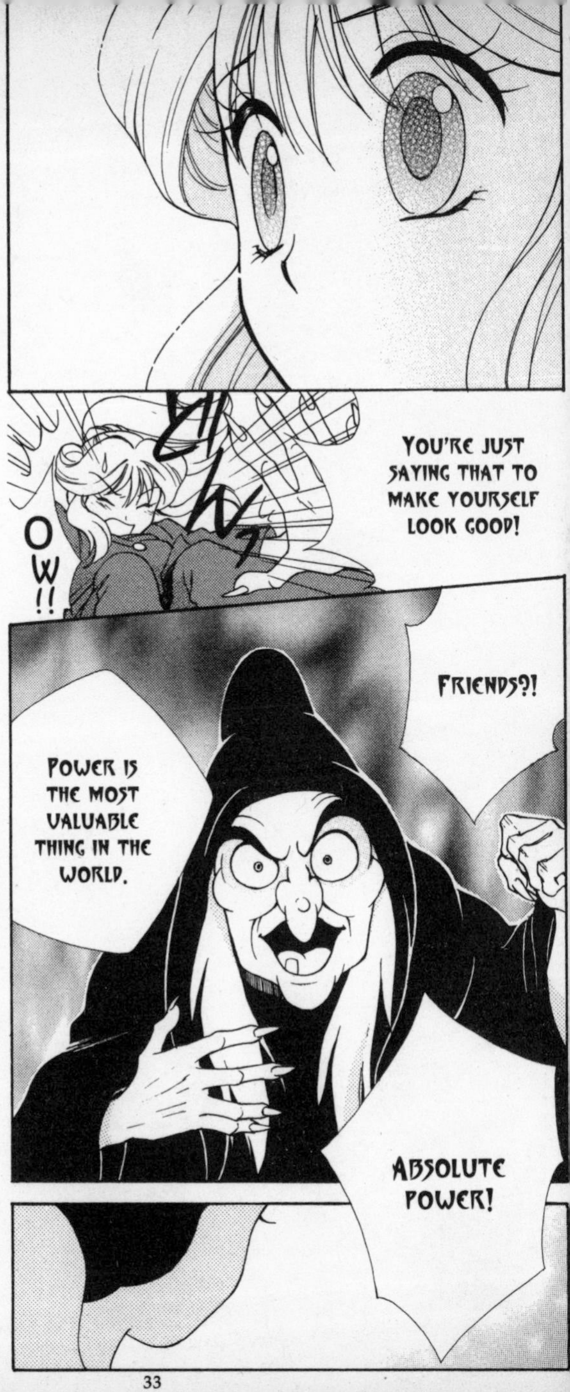

YOU'RE JUST SAYING THAT TO MAKE YOURSELF LOOK GOOD!
OW!!
FRIENDS?!
POWER IS THE MOST VALUABLE THING IN THE WORLD.
ABSOLUTE POWER!

Jasmine

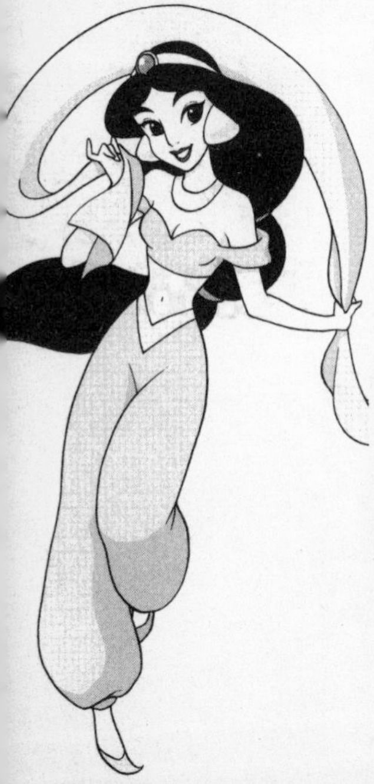

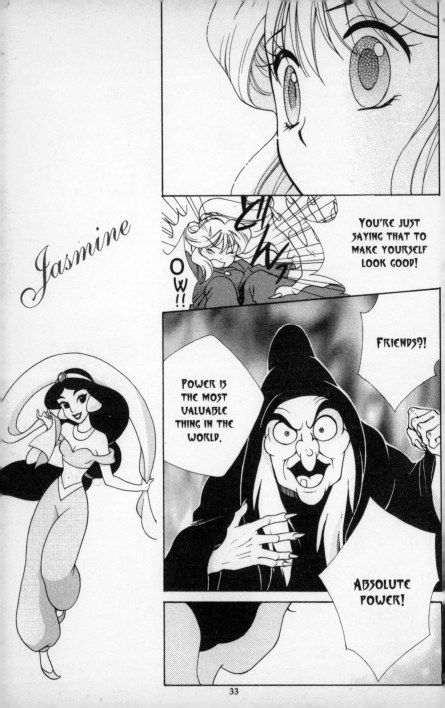

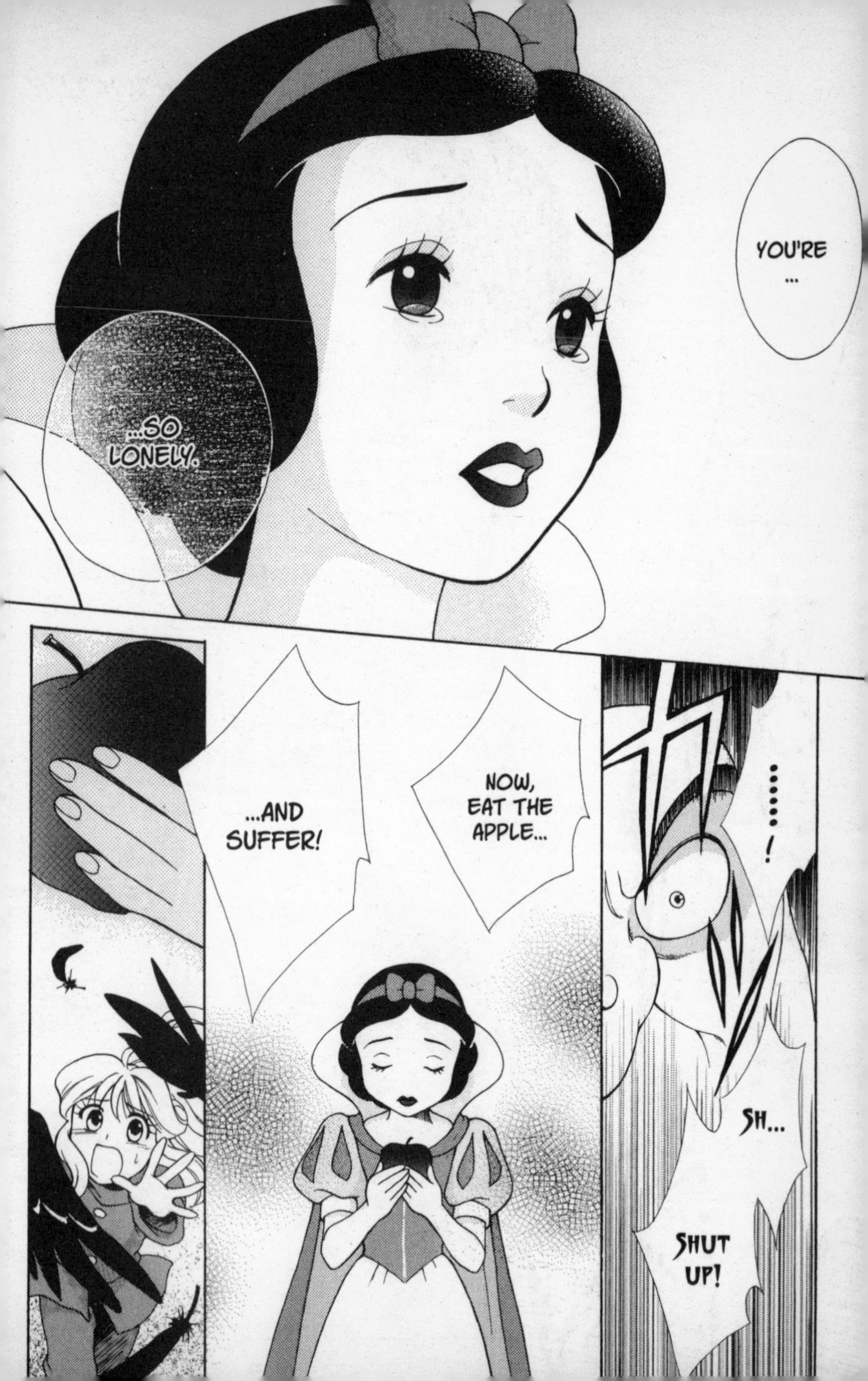
YOU'RE ...
...SO LONELY.
......!
SH...
SHUT UP!
NOW, EAT THE APPLE...
...AND SUFFER!

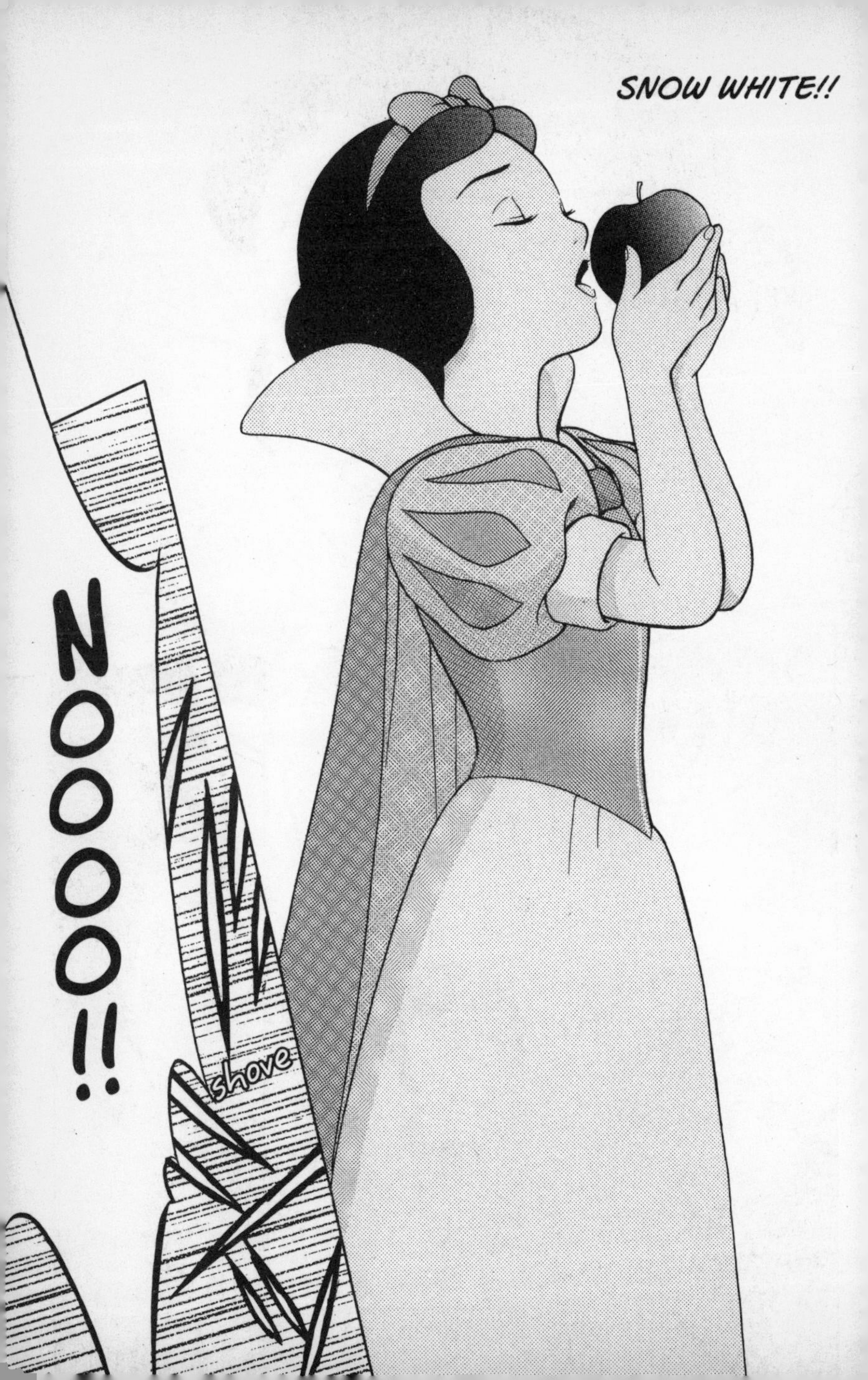
SNOW WHITE!!
NOOOO!!
shove

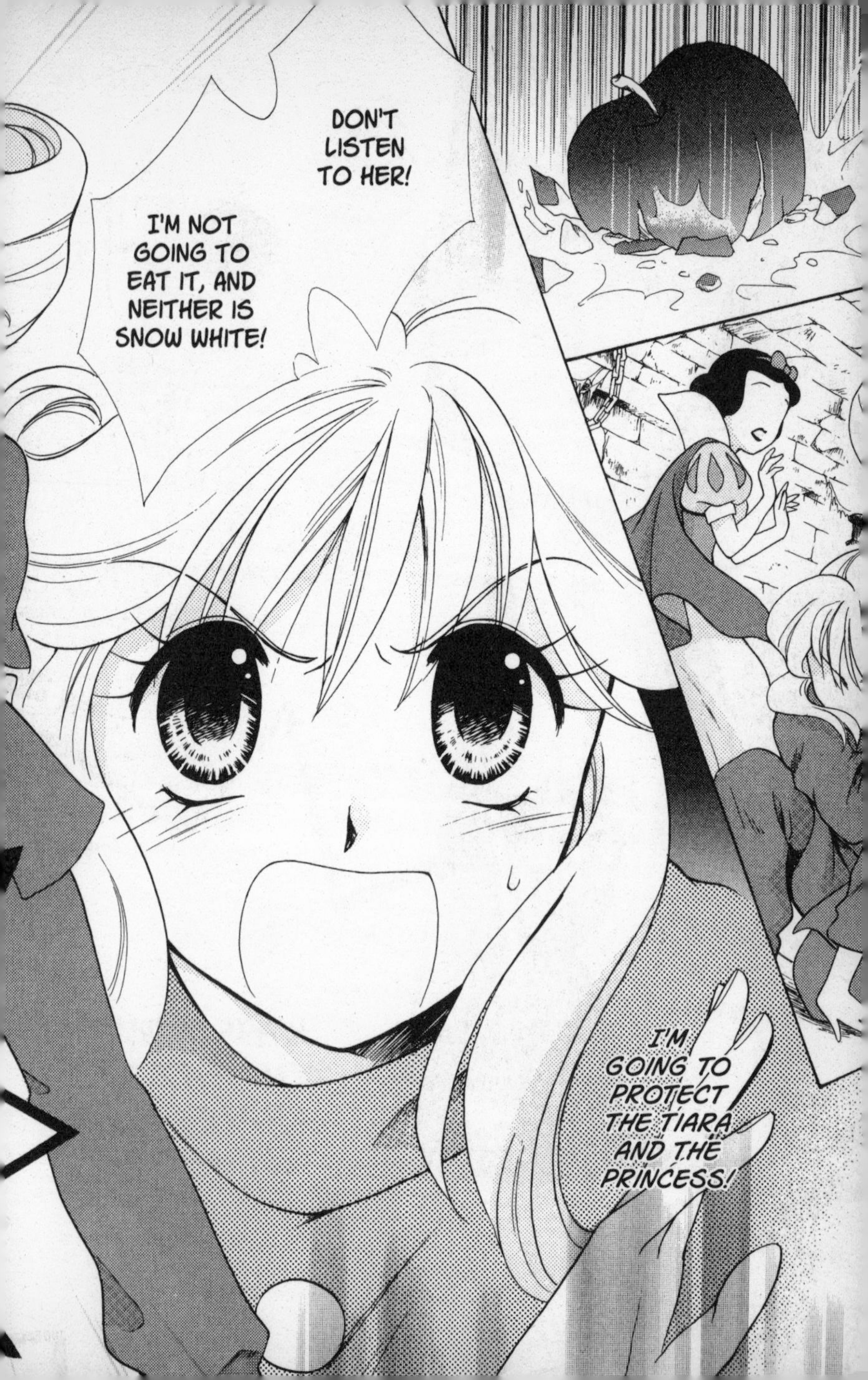
DON'T LISTEN TO HER!
I'M NOT GOING TO EAT IT, AND NEITHER IS SNOW WHITE!
I'M GOING TO PROTECT THE TIARA AND THE PRINCESS!

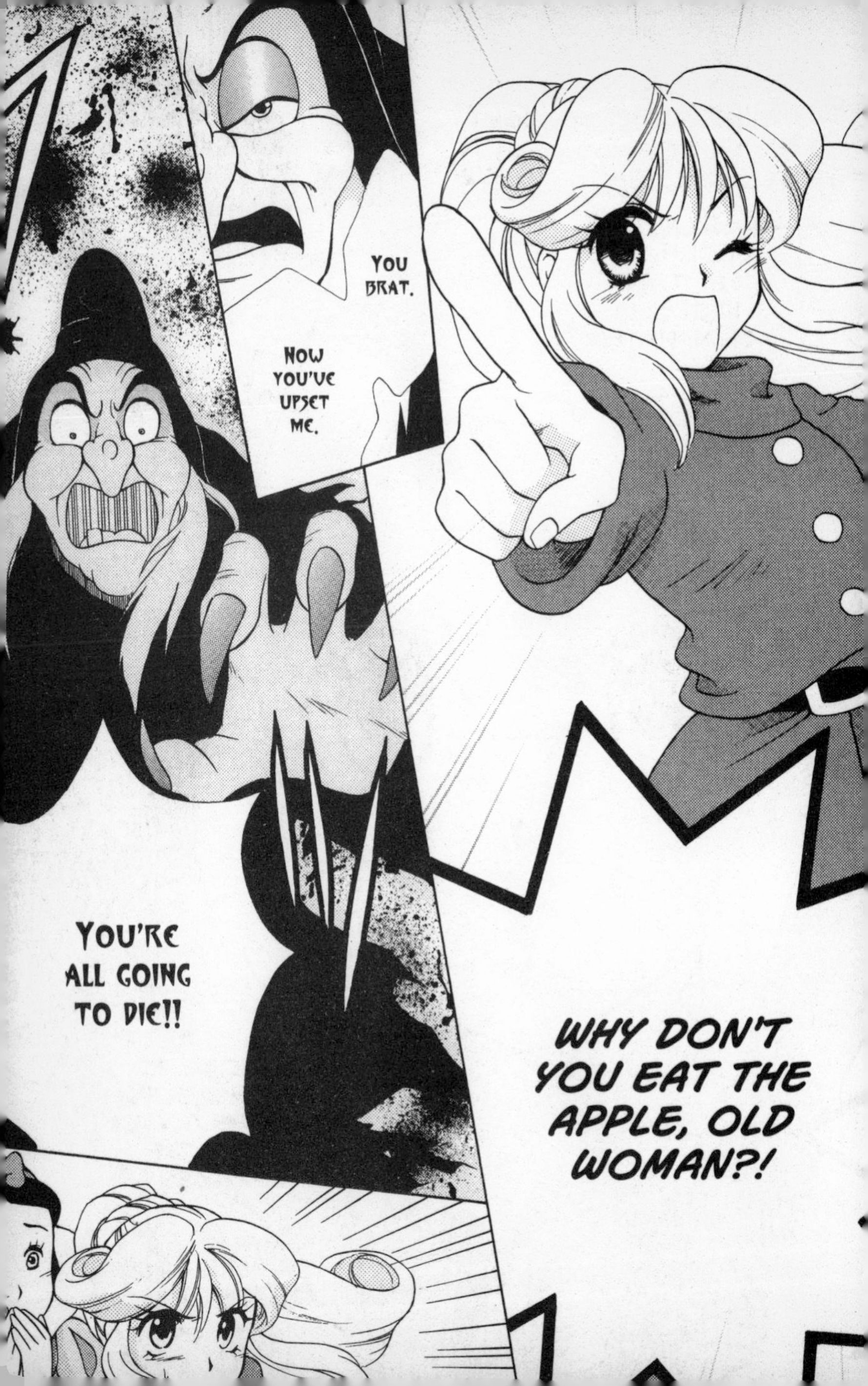
WHY DON'T YOU EAT THE APPLE, OLD WOMAN?!
YOU BRAT.
NOW YOU'VE UPSET ME.
YOU'RE ALL GOING TO DIE!!

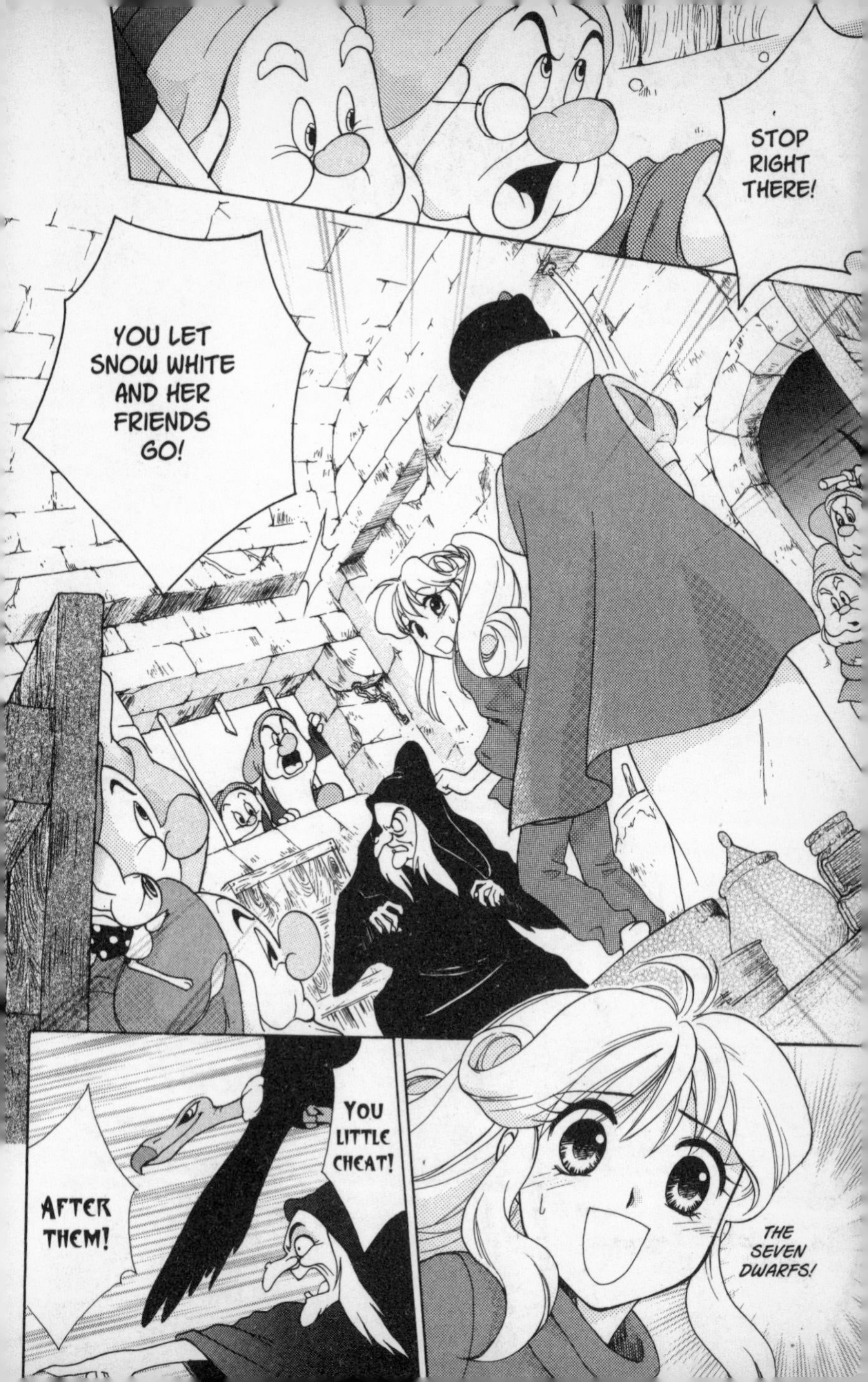
STOP RIGHT THERE!
YOU LET SNOW WHITE AND HER FRIENDS GO!
THE SEVEN DWARFS!
YOU LITTLE CHEAT!
AFTER THEM!

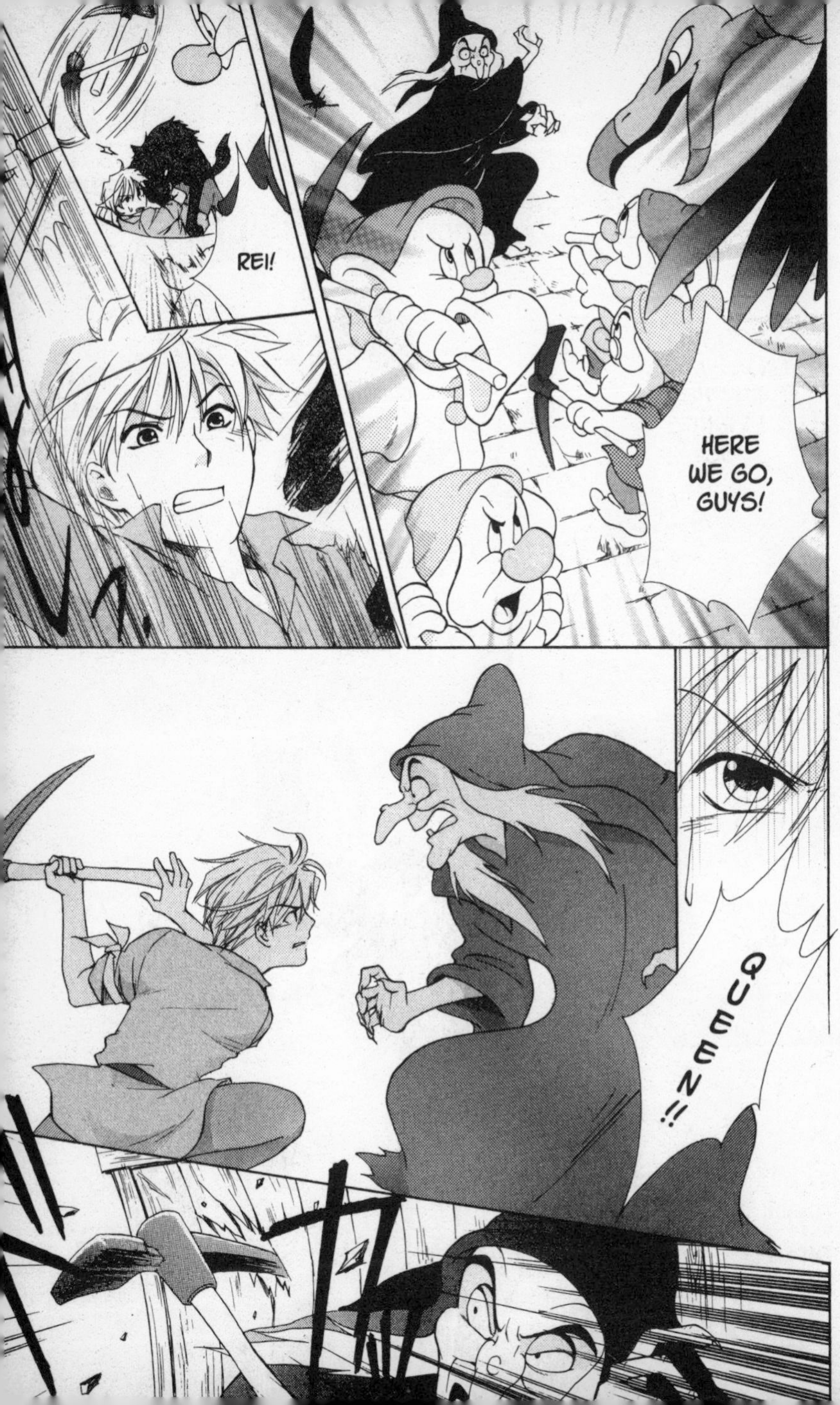
HERE WE GO, GUYS!
REI!
QUEEN!!

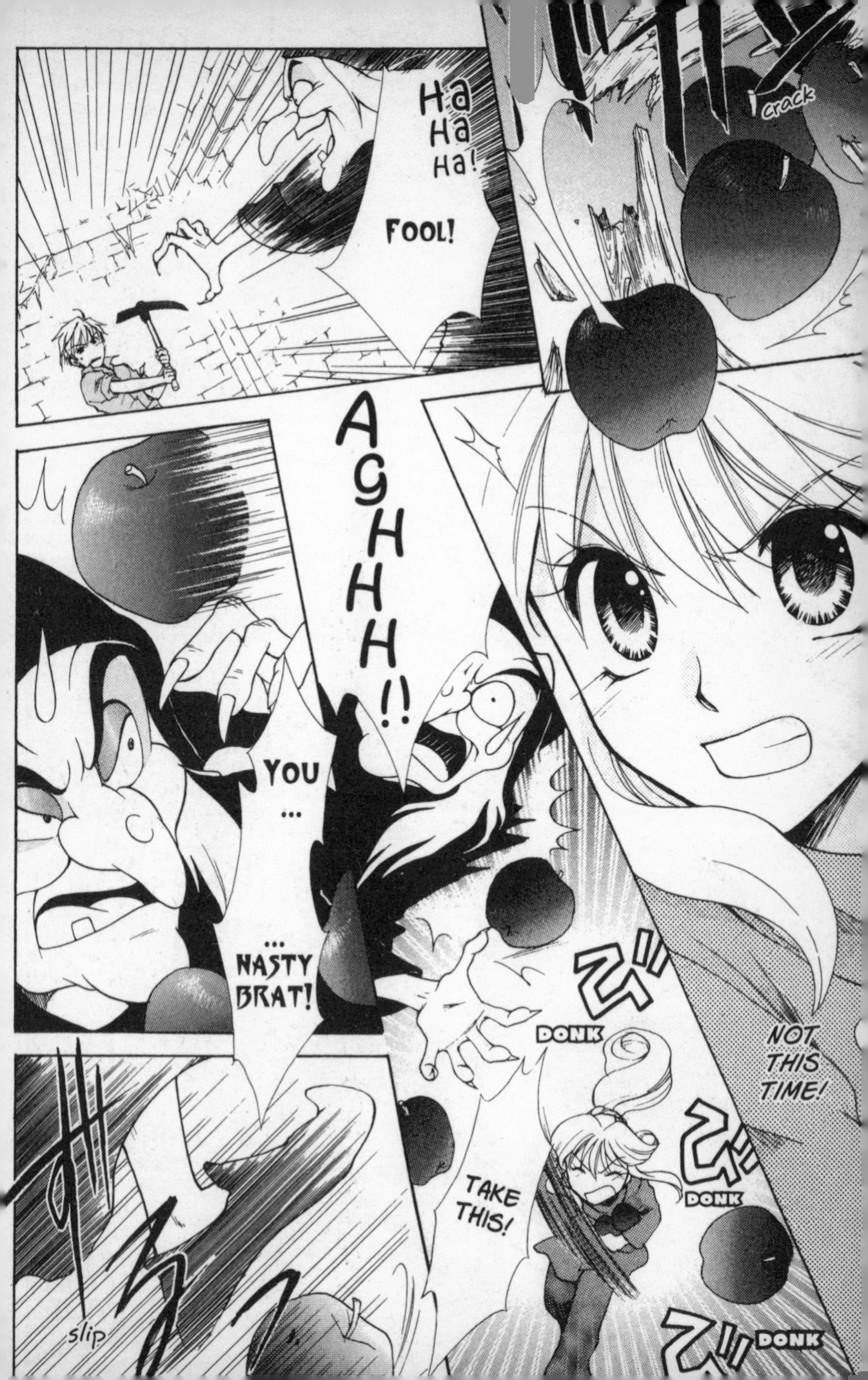
crack
Ha Ha Ha!
FOOL!
NOT THIS TIME!
AGHHH!!
YOU ...
... NASTY BRAT!
DONK
DONK
DONK
TAKE THIS!
slip

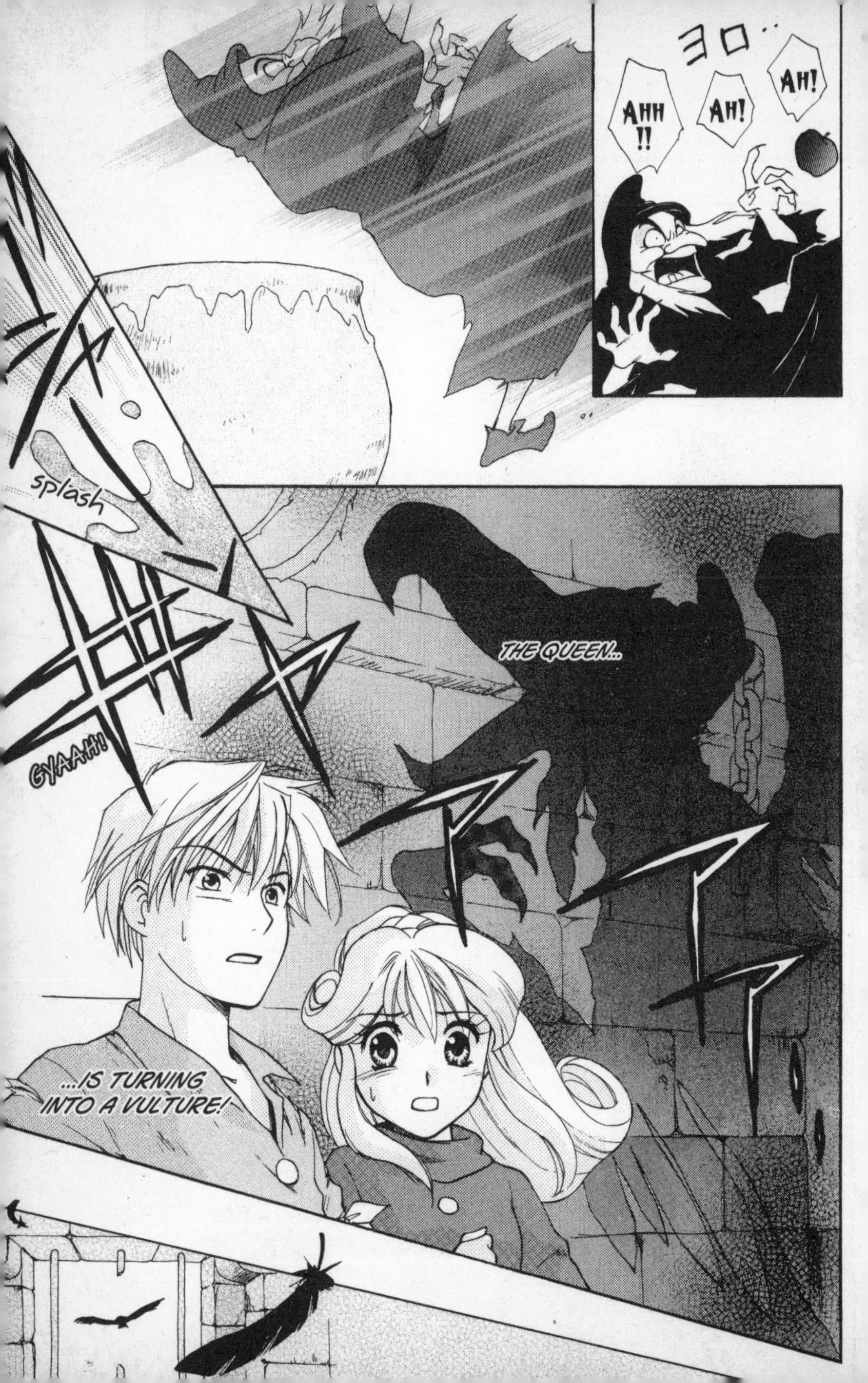
ヨロ..
AH!
AH!
AHH !!
splash
THE QUEEN...
GYAAH!
...IS TURNING INTO A VULTURE!

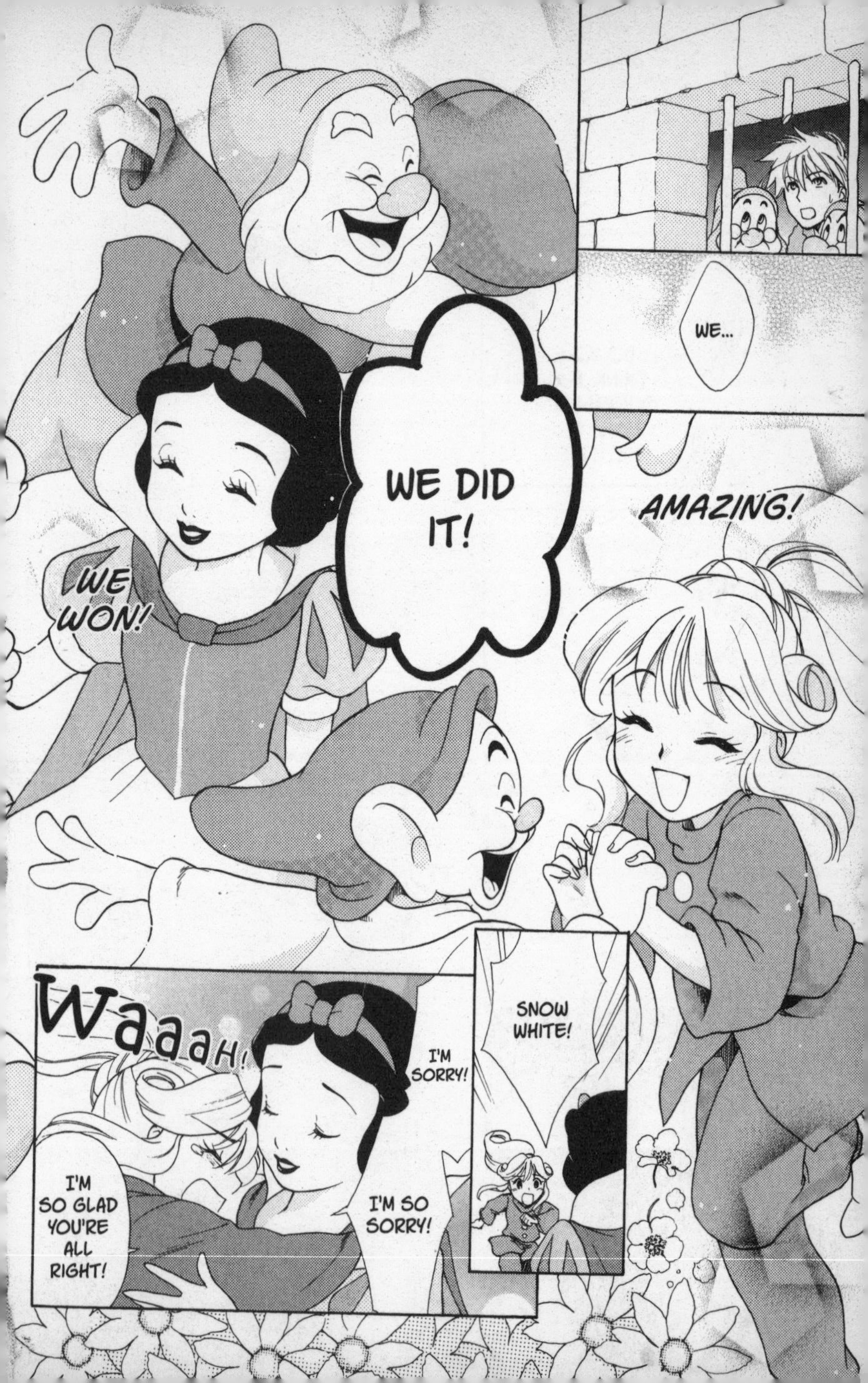
WE...
AMAZING!
WE DID IT!
WE WON!
SNOW WHITE!
Waaaah!
I'M SORRY!
I'M SO SORRY!
I'M SO GLAD YOU'RE ALL RIGHT!

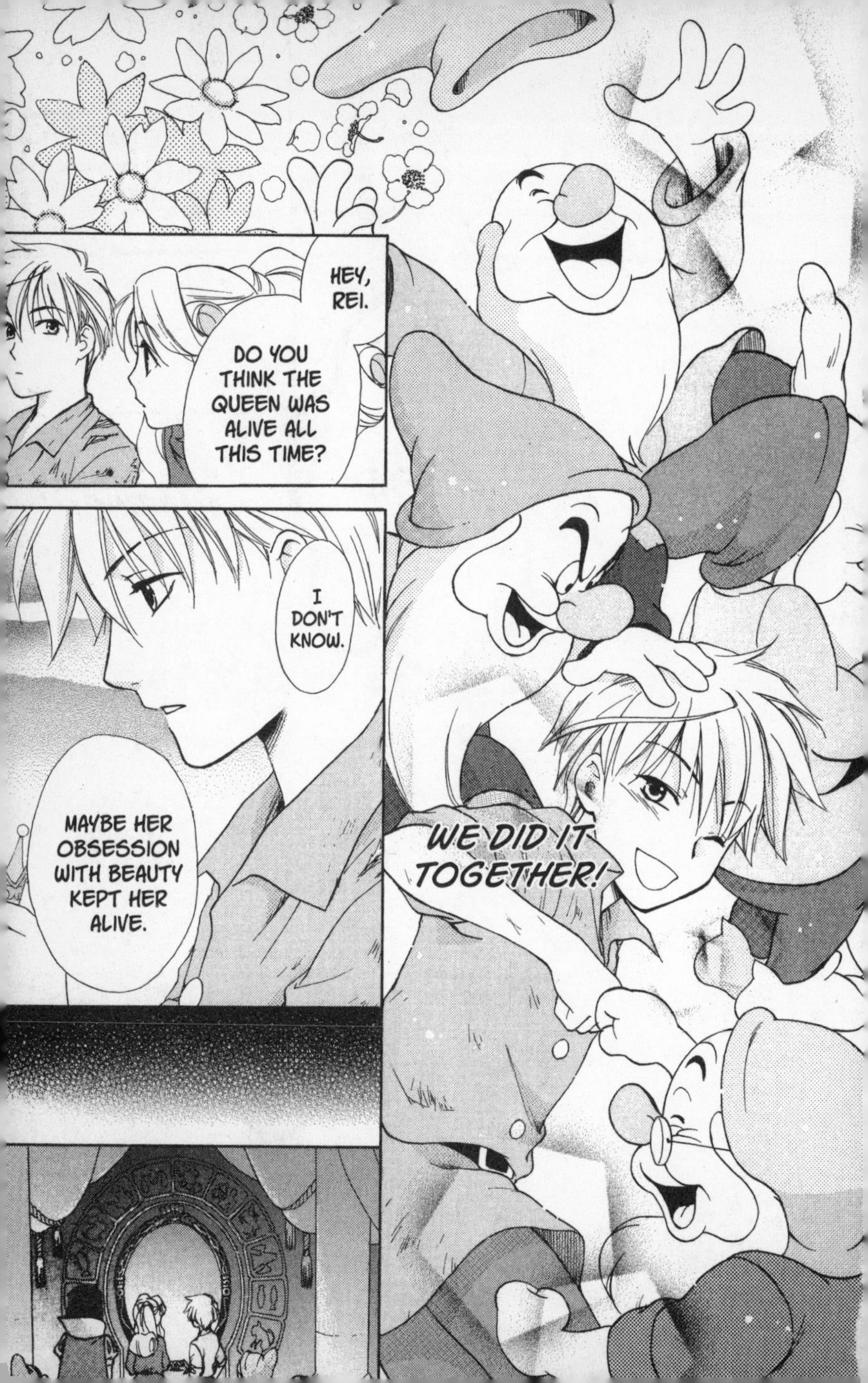
WE DID IT TOGETHER!
HEY, REI.
DO YOU THINK THE QUEEN WAS ALIVE ALL THIS TIME?
I DON'T KNOW.
MAYBE HER OBSESSION WITH BEAUTY KEPT HER ALIVE.

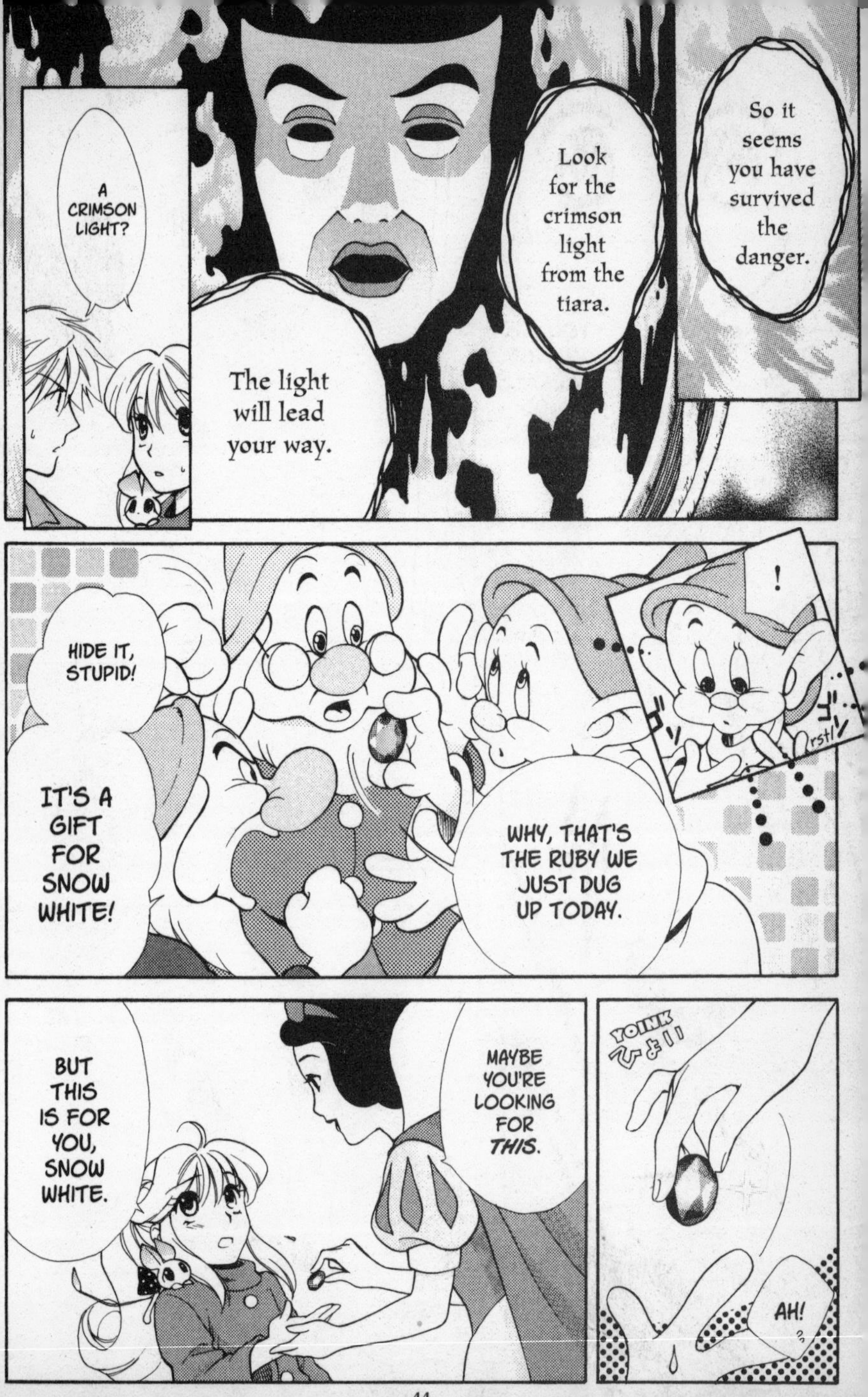

So it seems you have survived the danger.
Look for the crimson light from the tiara.
The light will lead your way.
A CRIMSON LIGHT?
!
rstl
WHY, THAT'S THE RUBY WE JUST DUG UP TODAY.
HIDE IT, STUPID!
IT'S A GIFT FOR SNOW WHITE!
YOINK
AH!
MAYBE YOU'RE LOOKING FOR *THIS*.
BUT THIS IS FOR YOU, SNOW WHITE.

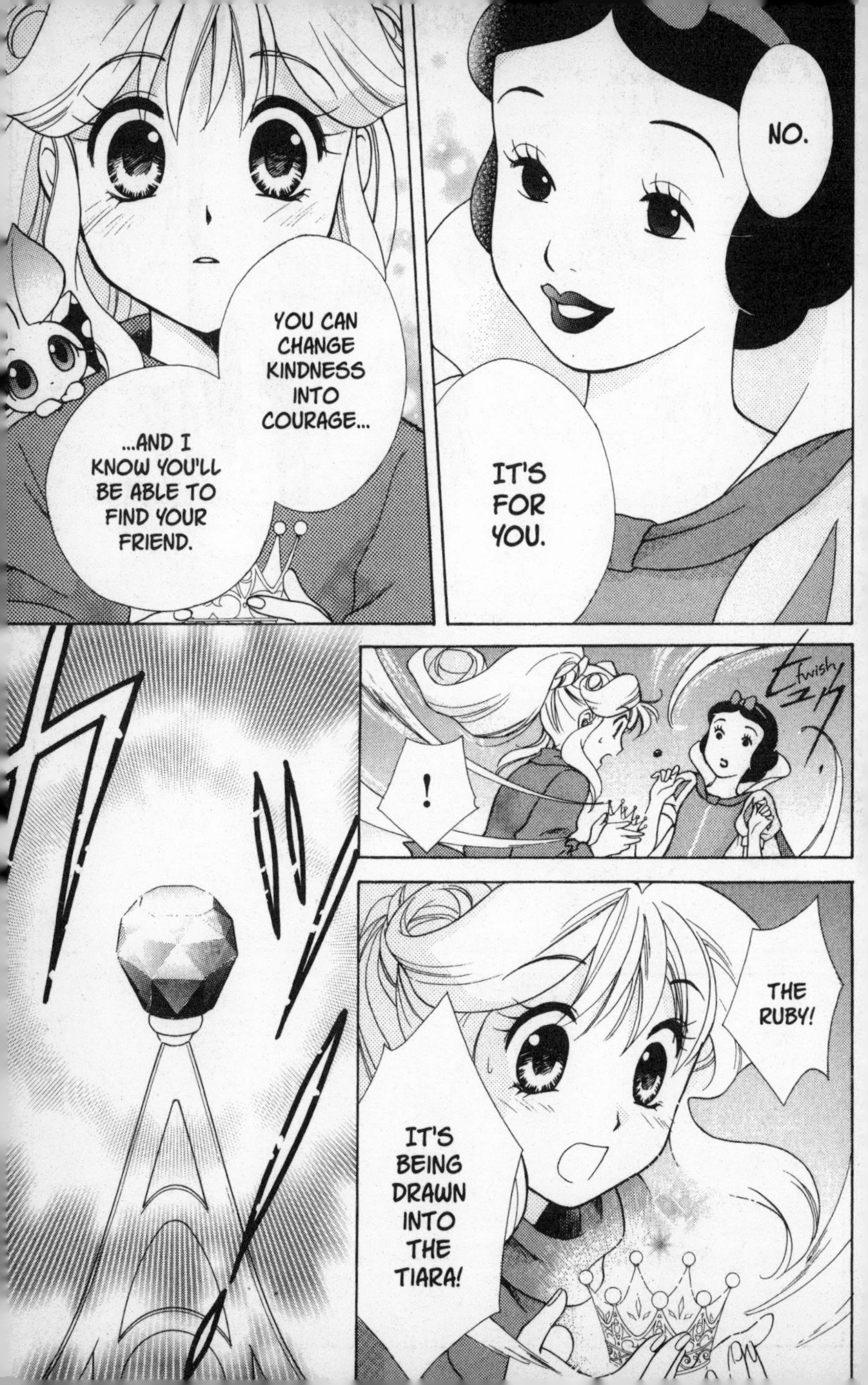
NO.
IT'S FOR YOU.
YOU CAN CHANGE KINDNESS INTO COURAGE...
...AND I KNOW YOU'LL BE ABLE TO FIND YOUR FRIEND.
twish
!
THE RUBY!
IT'S BEING DRAWN INTO THE TIARA!

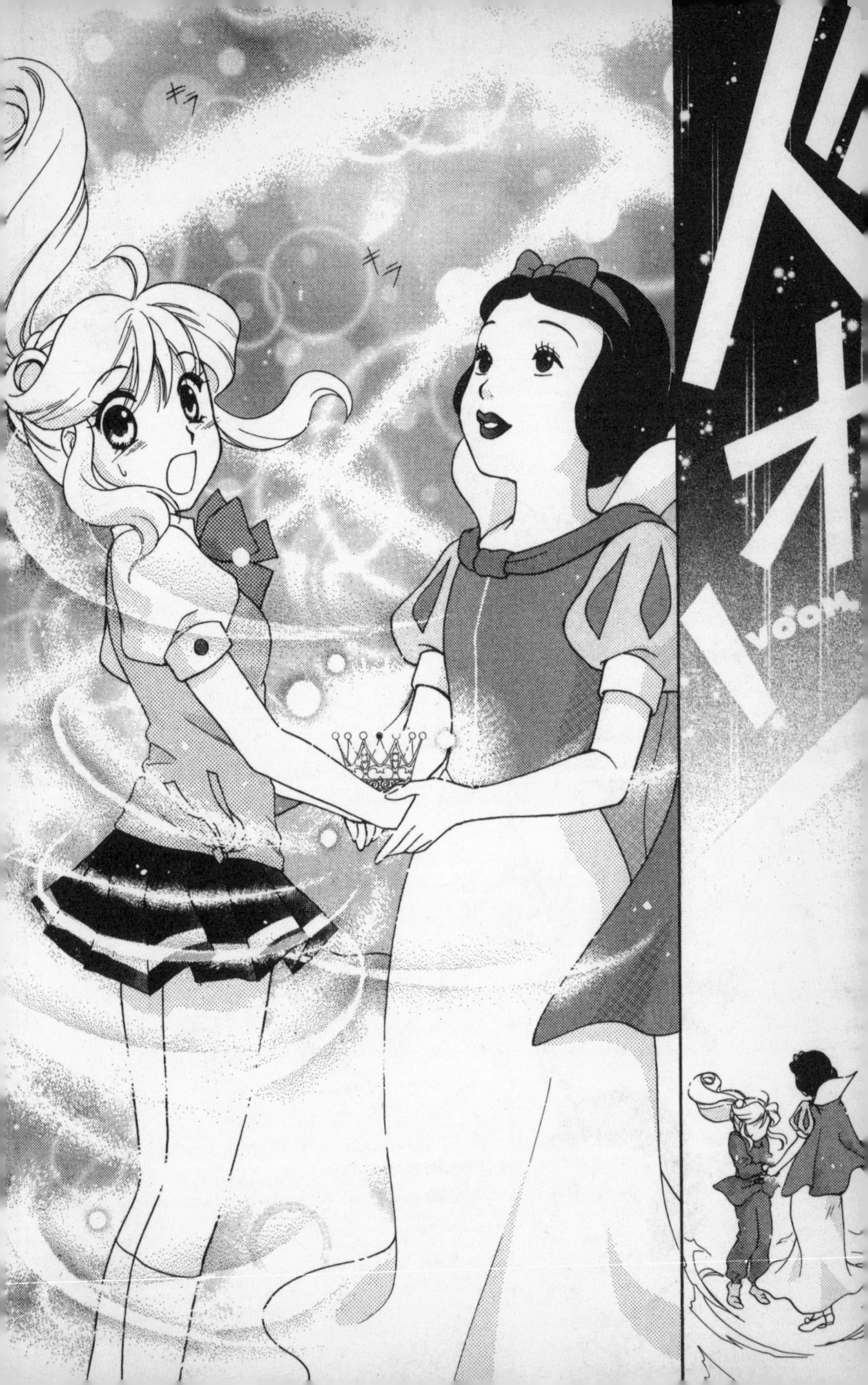
ドオー
VOOM
キラ
キラ

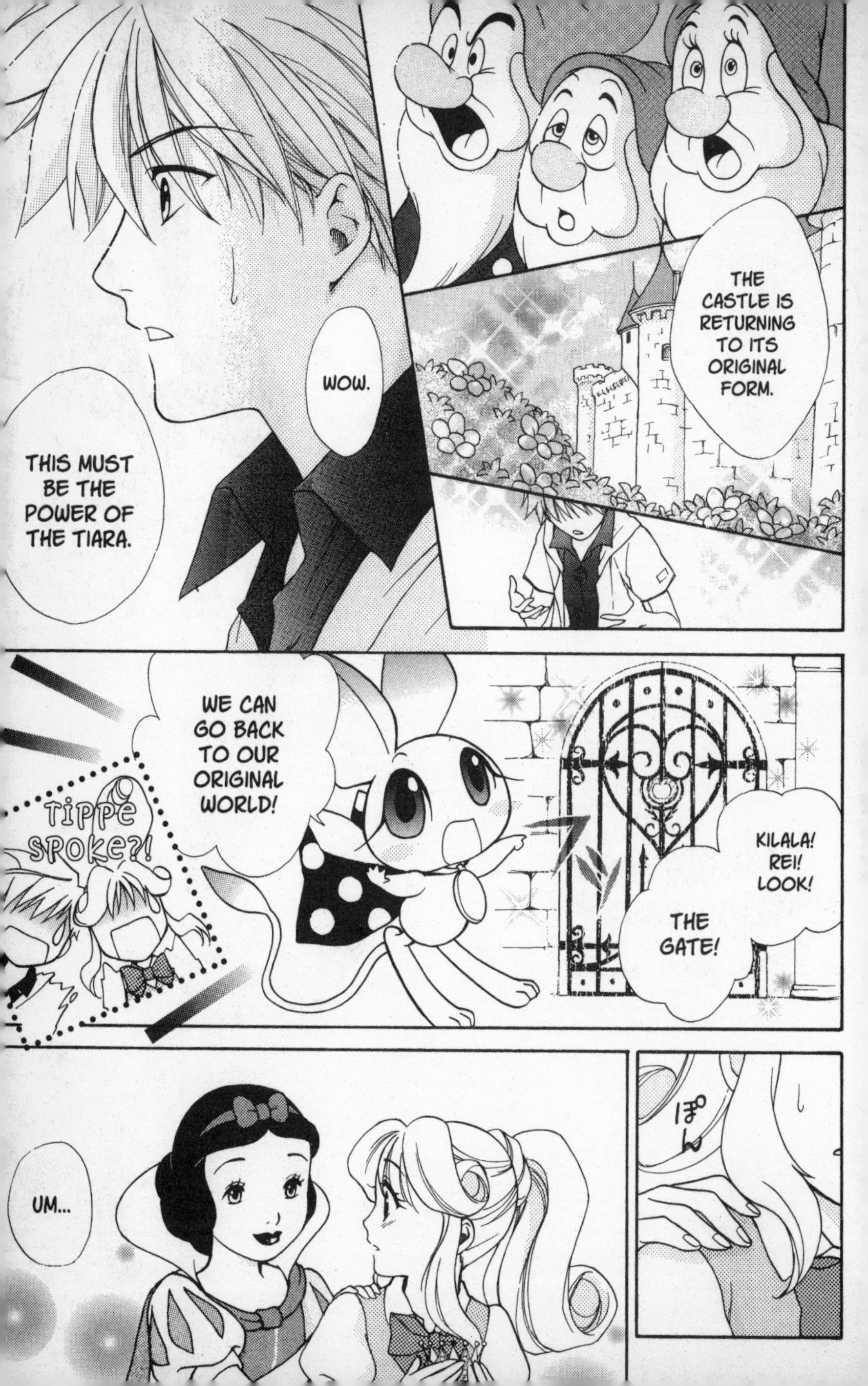
THE CASTLE IS RETURNING TO ITS ORIGINAL FORM.
WOW.
THIS MUST BE THE POWER OF THE TIARA.
KILALA! REI! LOOK!
THE GATE!
WE CAN GO BACK TO OUR ORIGINAL WORLD!
TIPPE SPOKE?!
ぽん
UM...

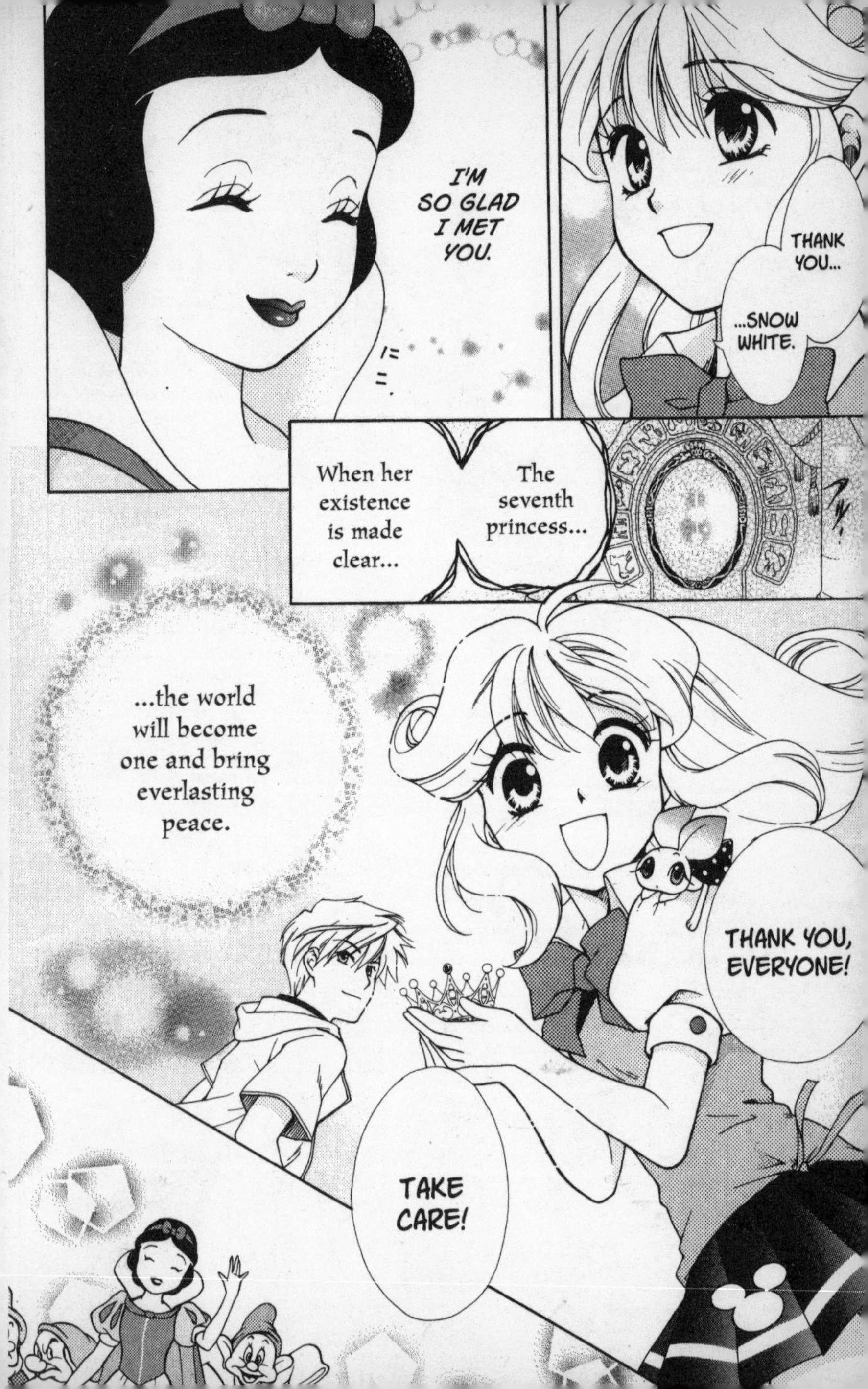
THANK YOU...
...SNOW WHITE.
I'M SO GLAD I MET YOU.
The seventh princess...
When her existence is made clear...
...the world will become one and bring everlasting peace.
THANK YOU, EVERYONE!
TAKE CARE!

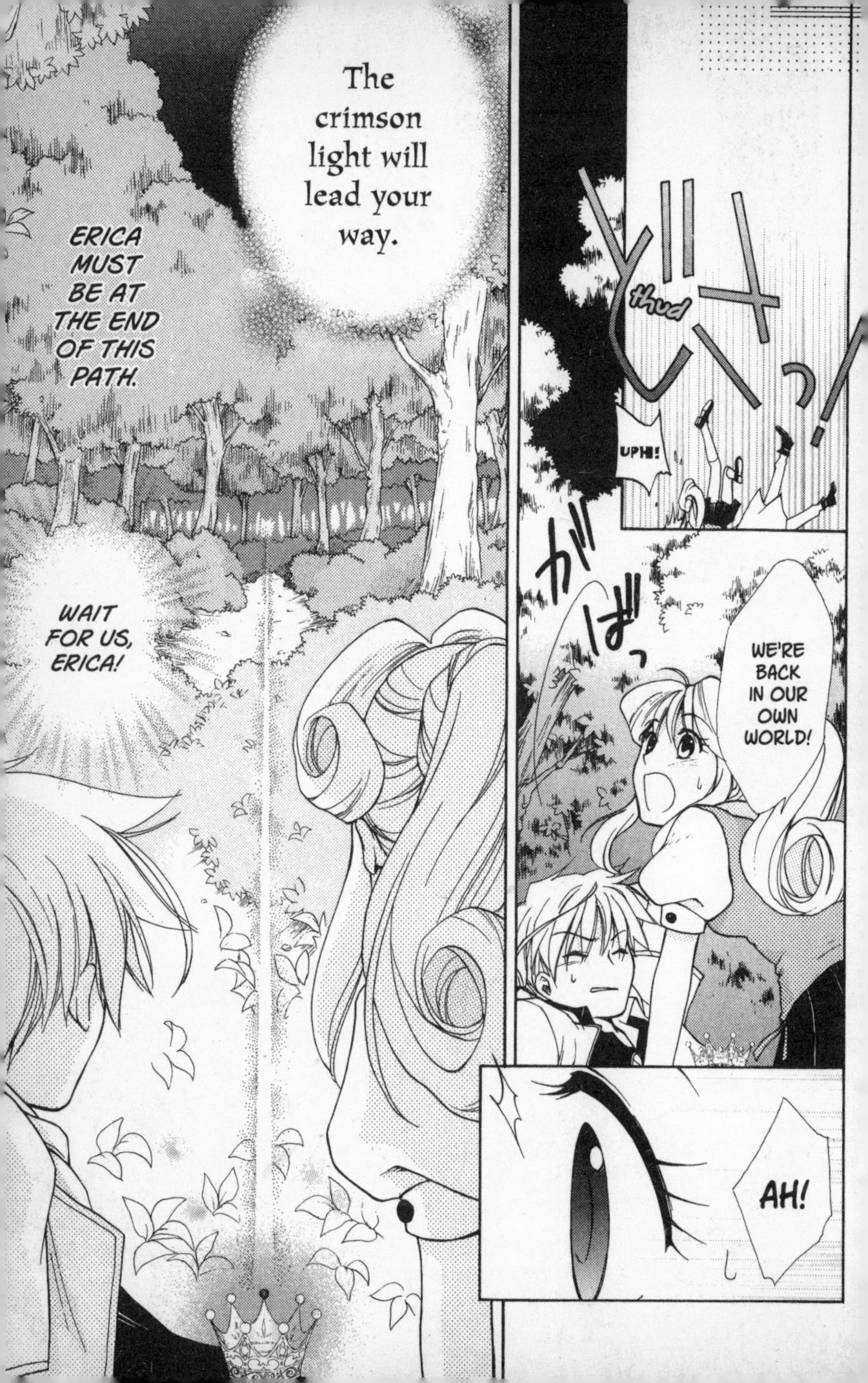
thud
UPH!
がばっ
WE'RE BACK IN OUR OWN WORLD!
AH!
The crimson light will lead your way.
ERICA MUST BE AT THE END OF THIS PATH.
WAIT FOR US, ERICA!

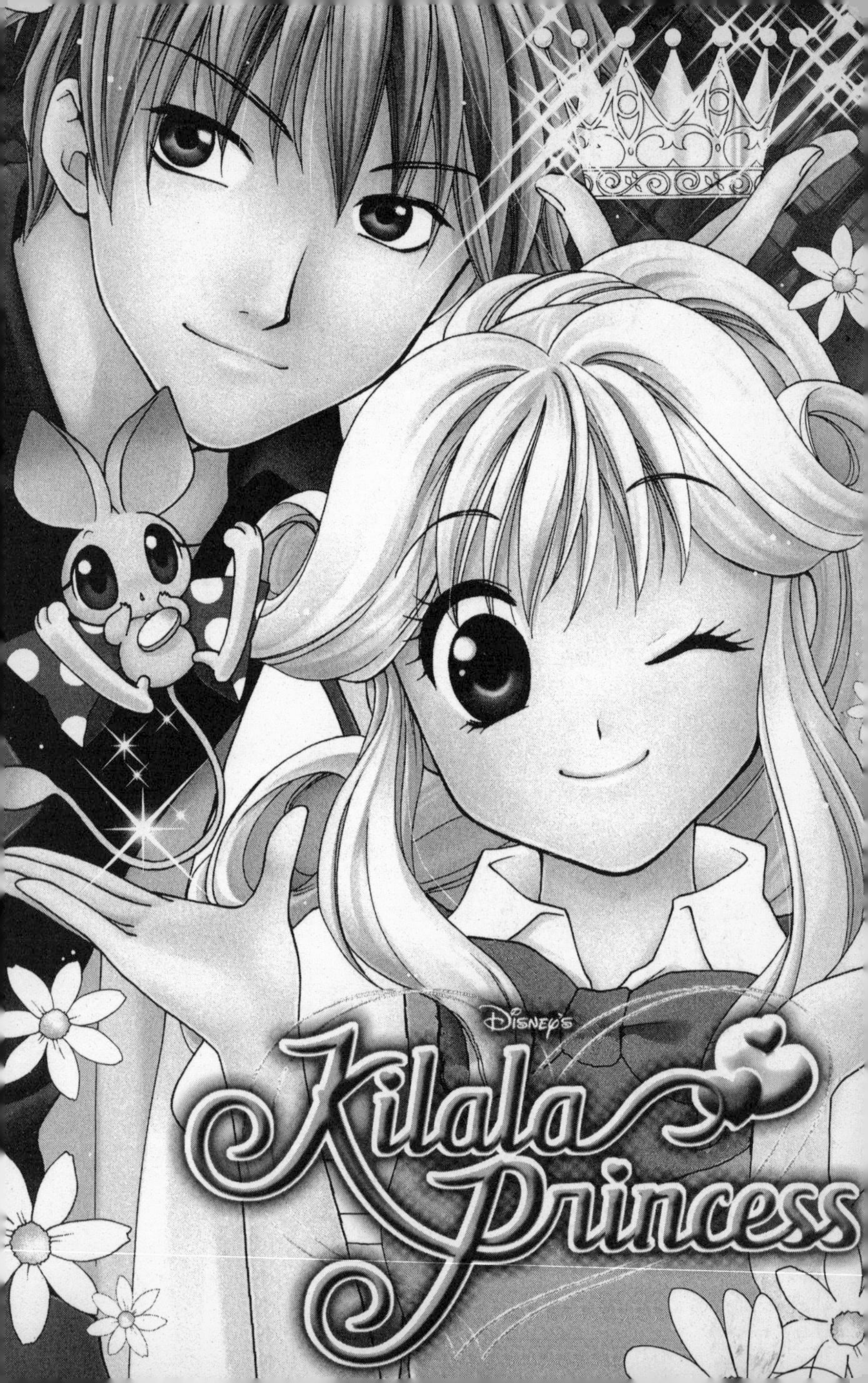
Disney's
Kilala Princess

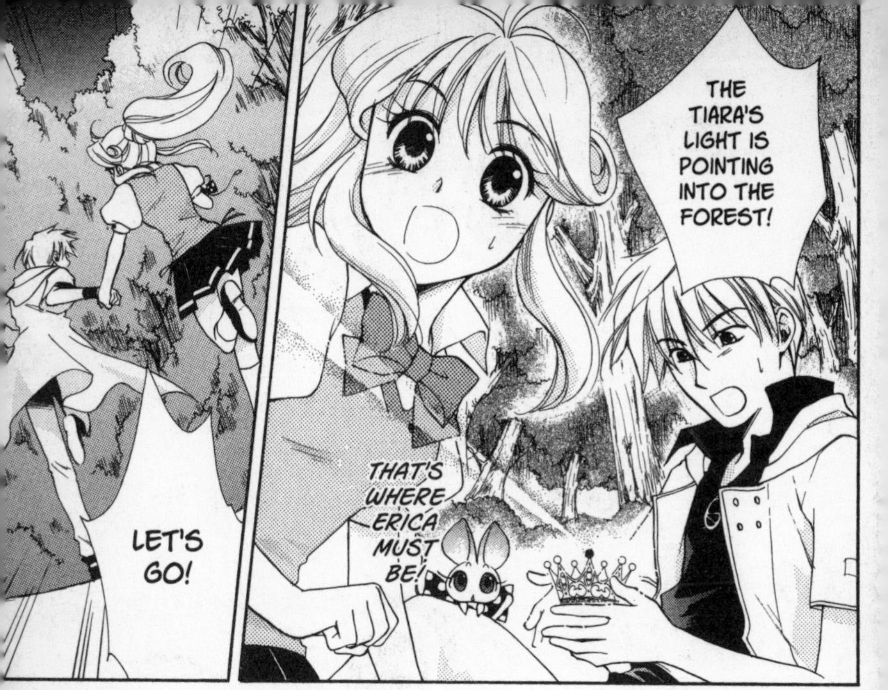
THE TIARA'S LIGHT IS POINTING INTO THE FOREST!
THAT'S WHERE ERICA MUST BE!
LET'S GO!

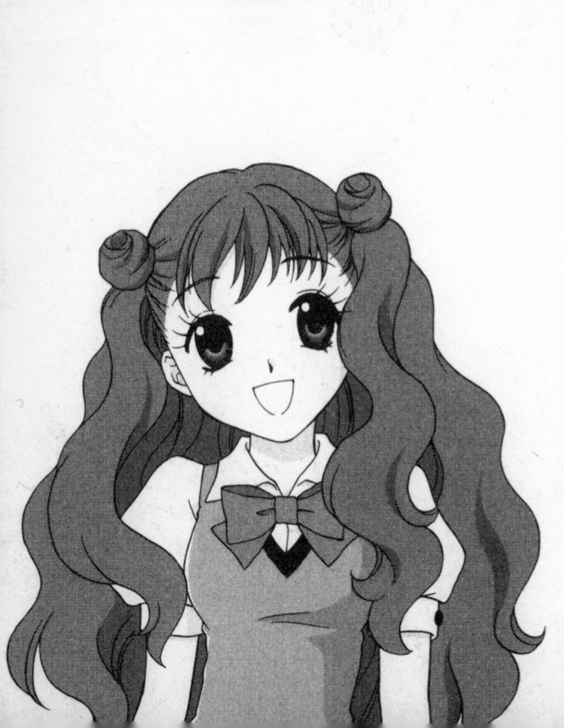

Erica

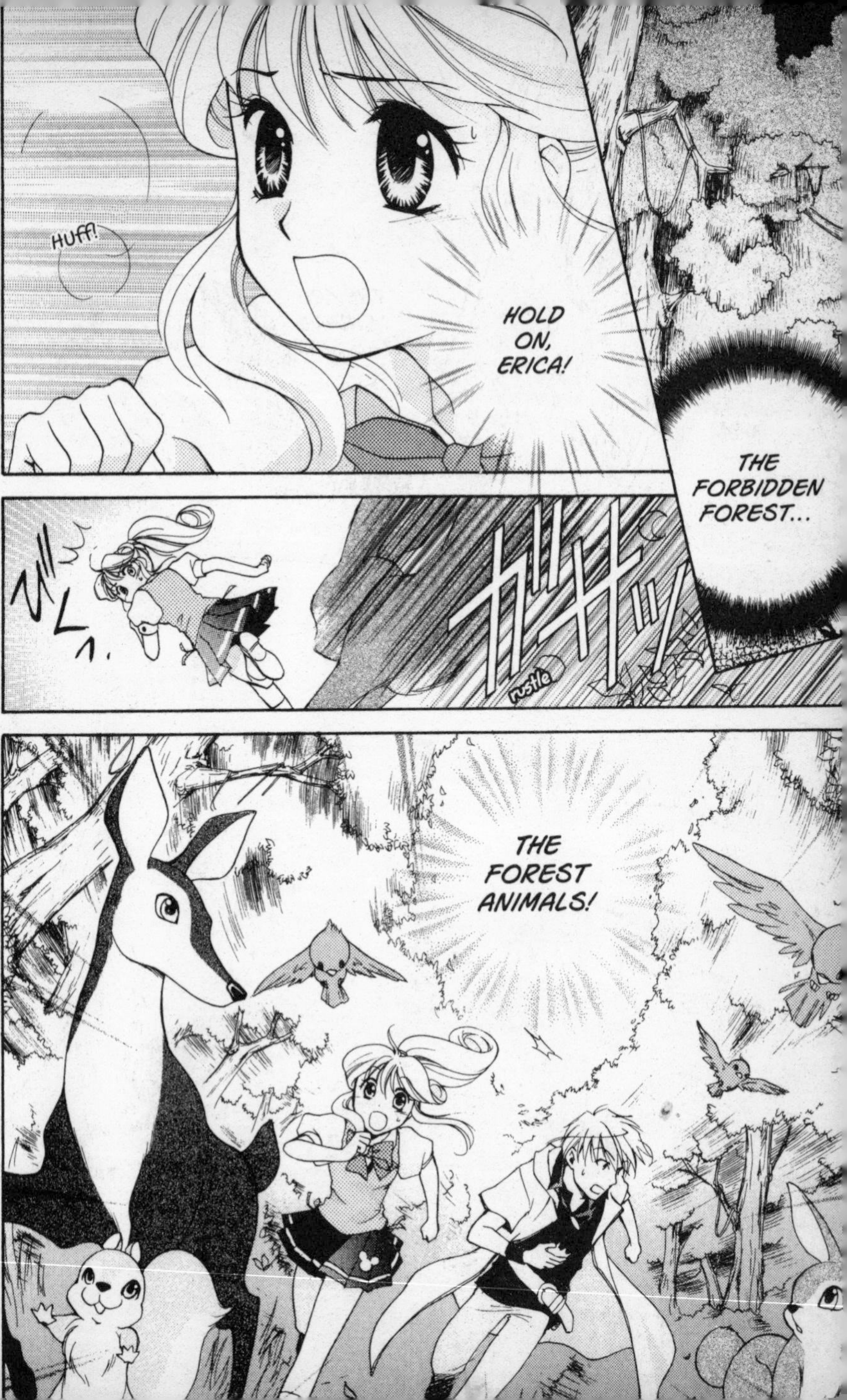
THE FORBIDDEN FOREST...
HOLD ON, ERICA!
HUFF!
rustle
THE FOREST ANIMALS!

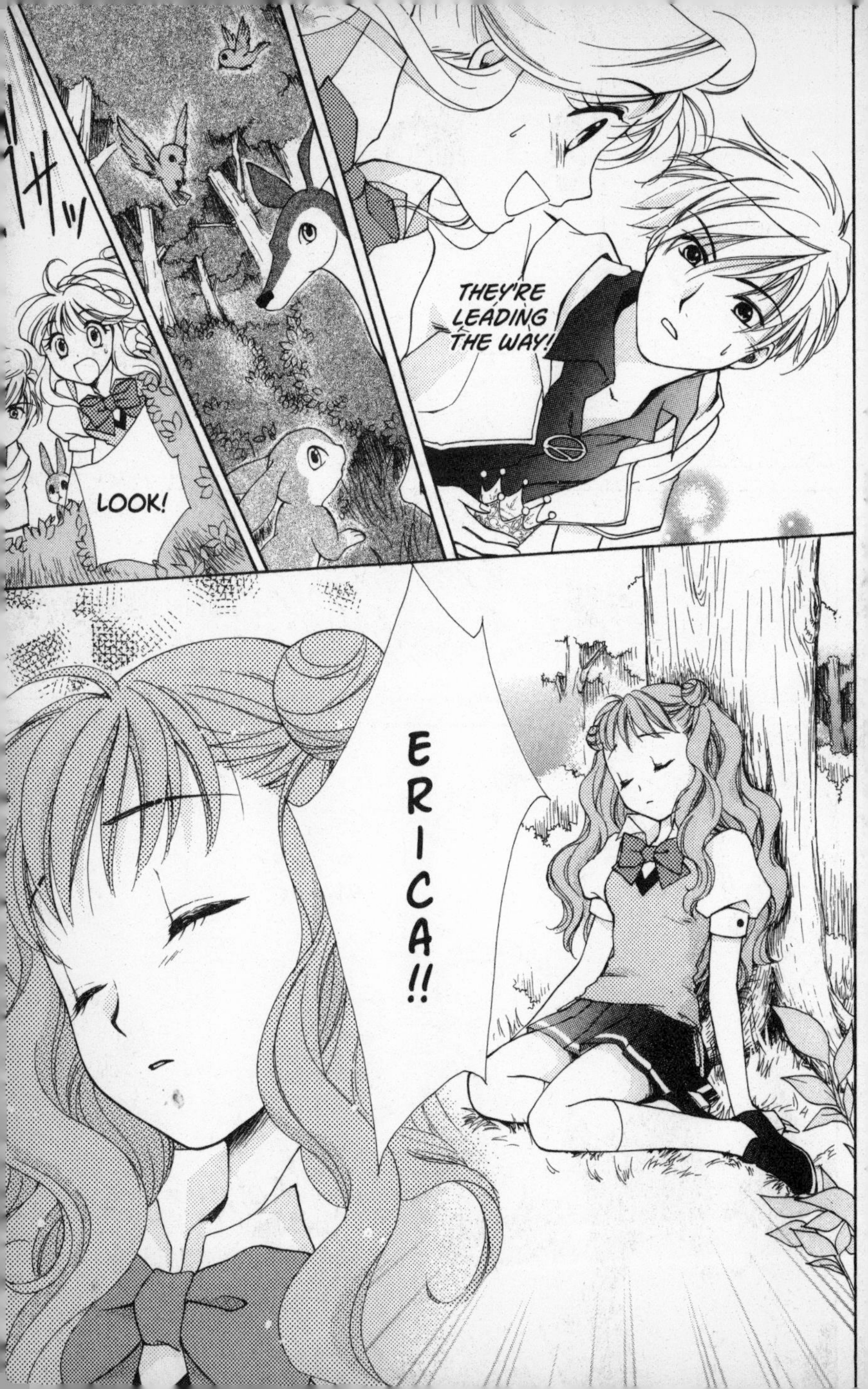
THEY'RE LEADING THE WAY!
LOOK!
ERICA!!

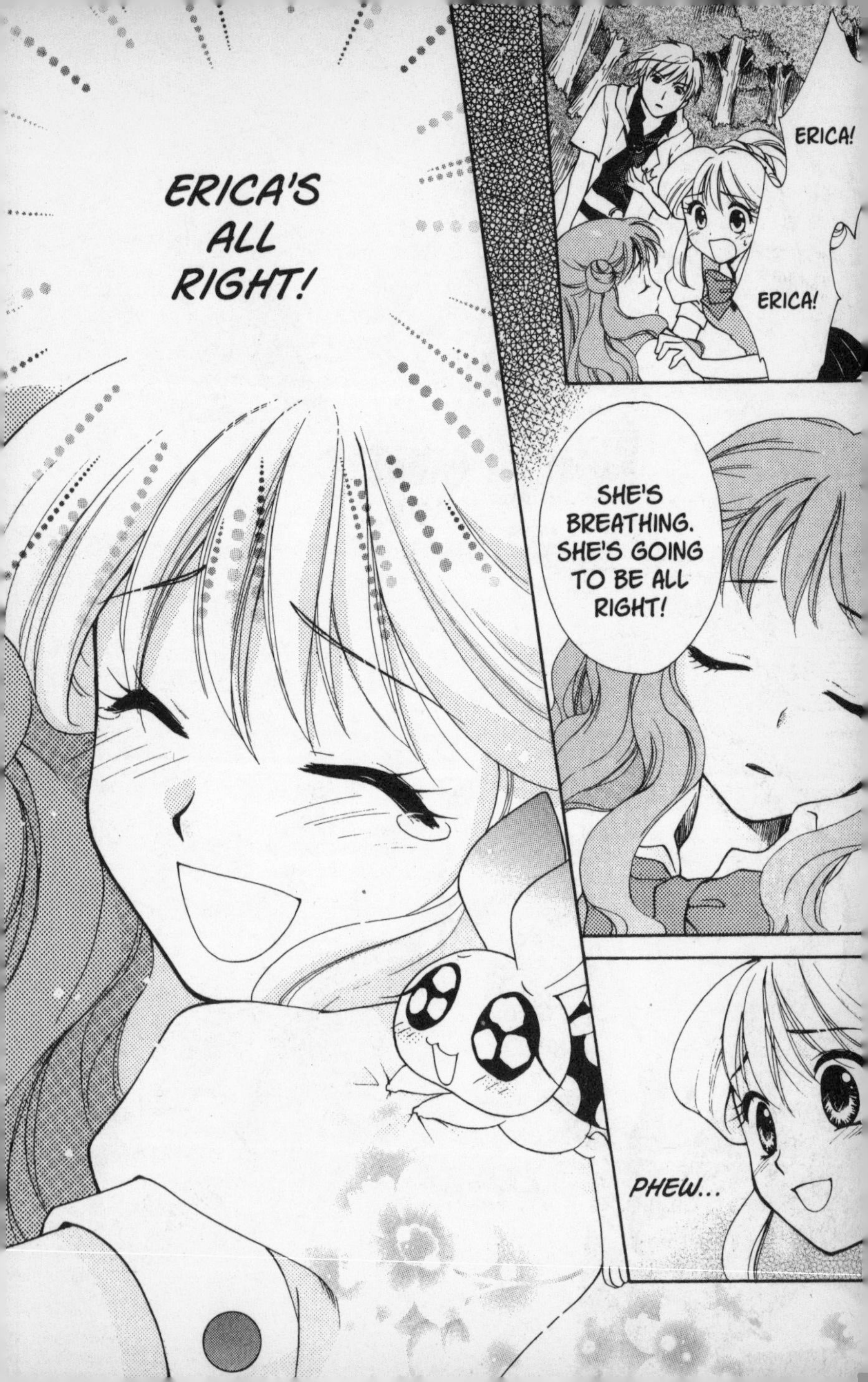
ERICA!
ERICA!
SHE'S BREATHING. SHE'S GOING TO BE ALL RIGHT!
PHEW...
ERICA'S ALL RIGHT!

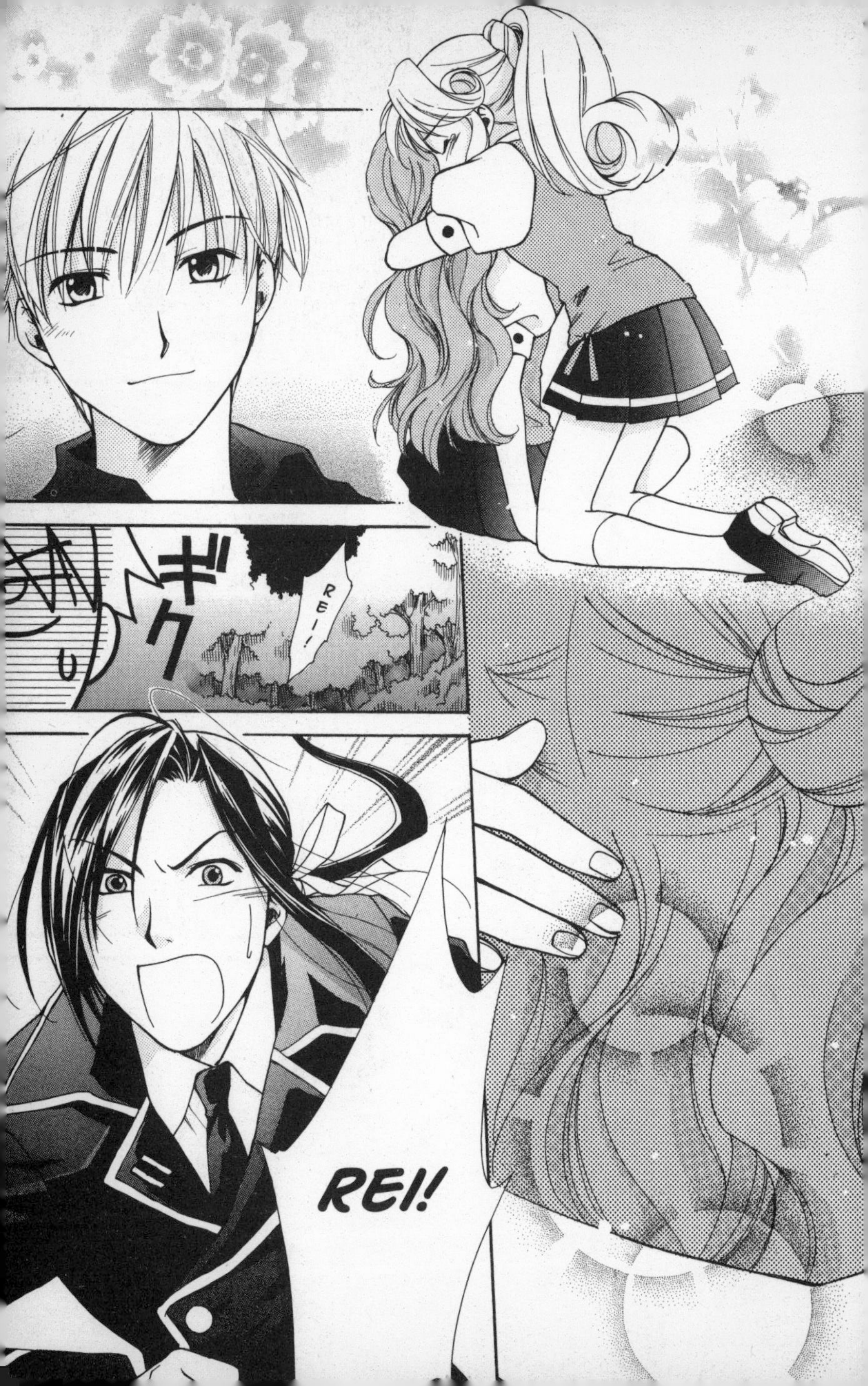
ギク
REI!
REI!

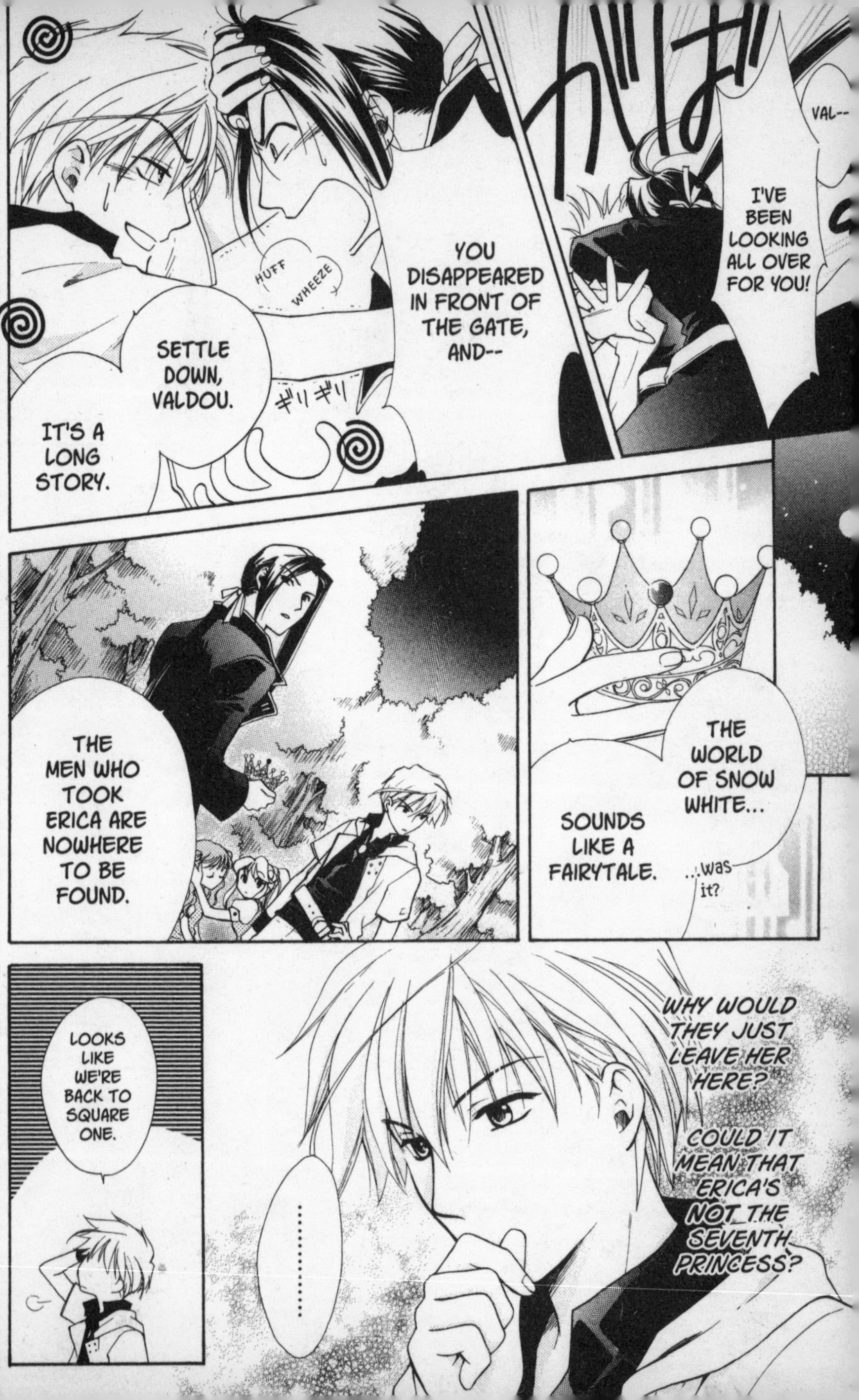
VAL--
I'VE BEEN LOOKING ALL OVER FOR YOU!
YOU DISAPPEARED IN FRONT OF THE GATE, AND--
HUFF
WHEEZE
SETTLE DOWN, VALDOU.
ギリギリ
IT'S A LONG STORY.
THE WORLD OF SNOW WHITE...
SOUNDS LIKE A FAIRYTALE.
...was it?
THE MEN WHO TOOK ERICA ARE NOWHERE TO BE FOUND.
WHY WOULD THEY JUST LEAVE HER HERE?
COULD IT MEAN THAT ERICA'S NOT THE SEVENTH PRINCESS?
......
LOOKS LIKE WE'RE BACK TO SQUARE ONE.

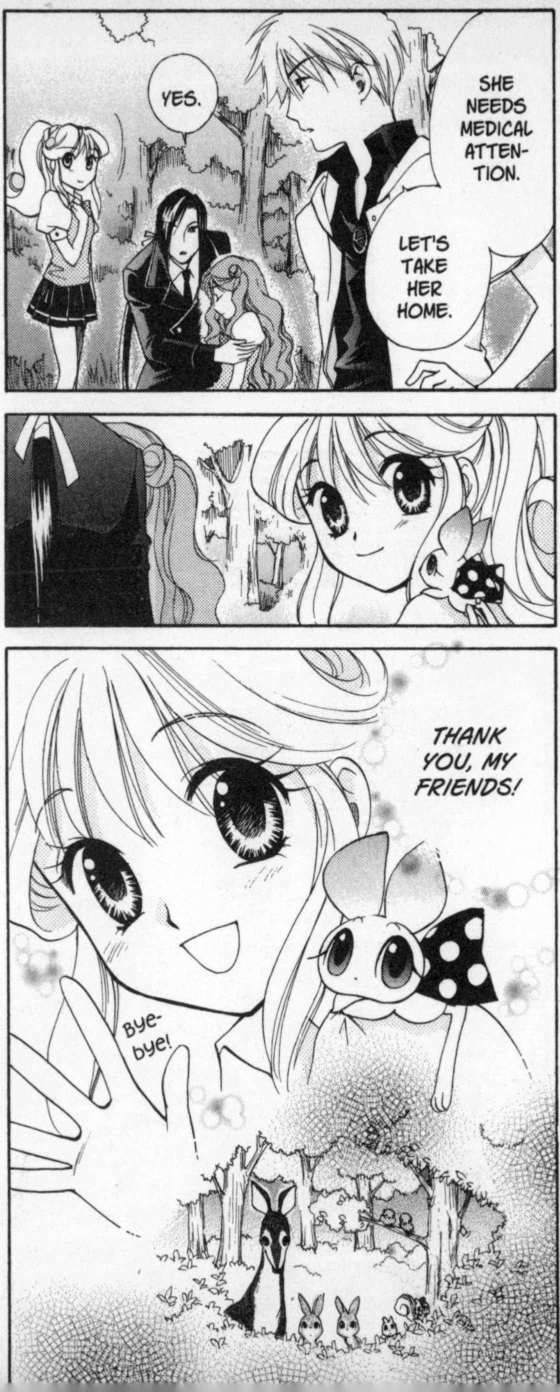
SHE NEEDS MEDICAL ATTEN- TION.
LET'S TAKE HER HOME.
YES.
THANK YOU, MY FRIENDS!
Bye-bye!

Belle

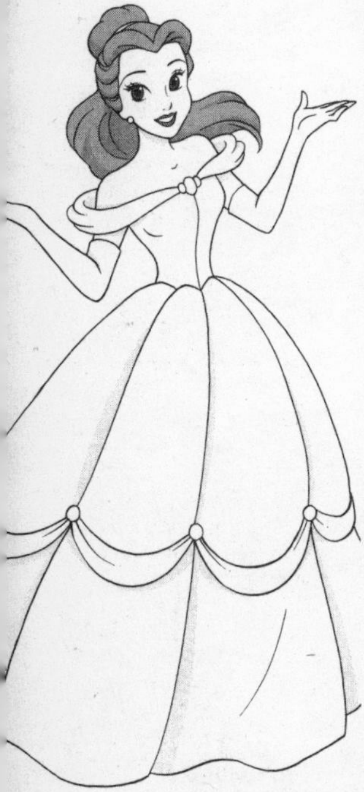

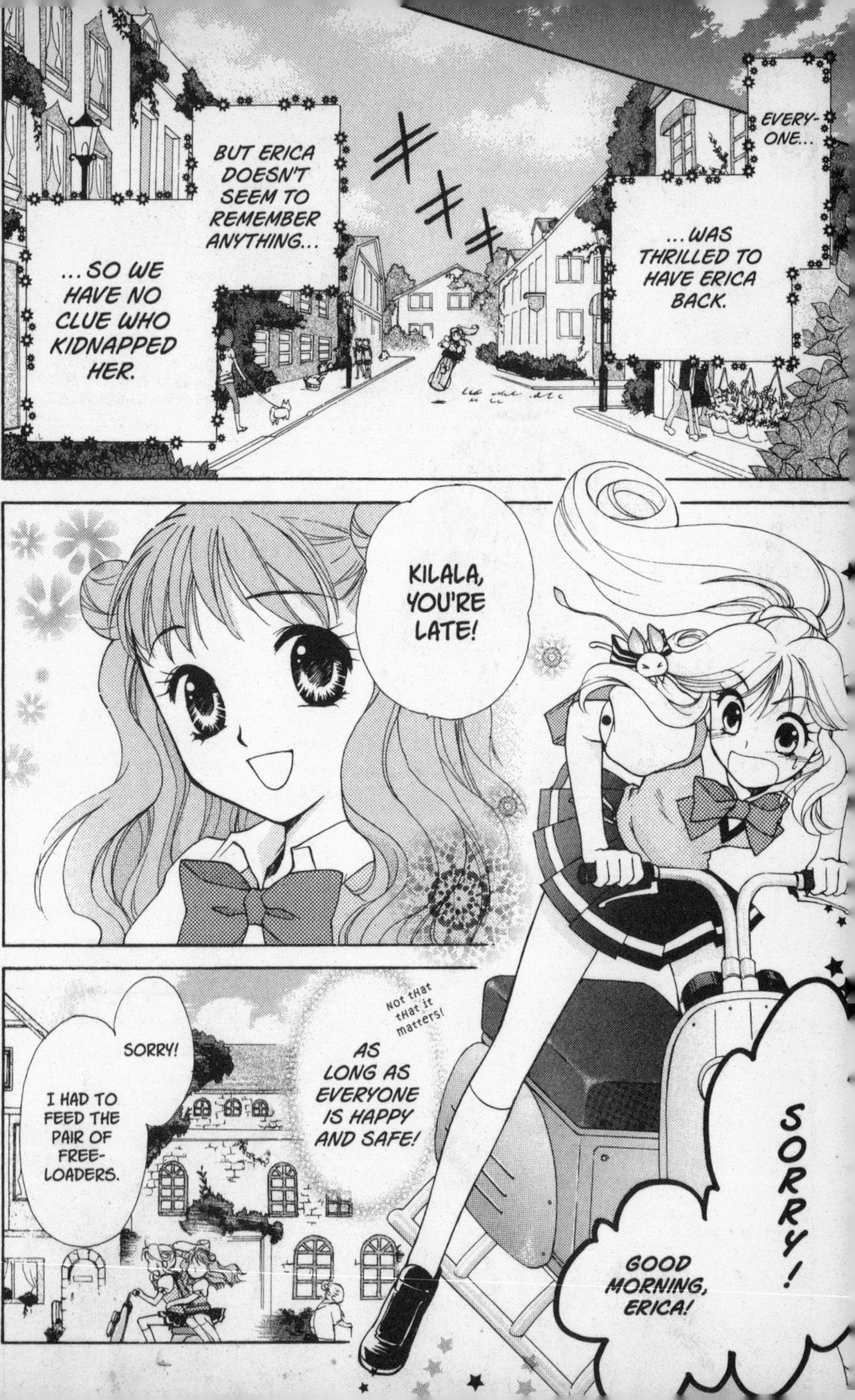
EVERY-ONE...
...WAS THRILLED TO HAVE ERICA BACK.
BUT ERICA DOESN'T SEEM TO REMEMBER ANYTHING...
...SO WE HAVE NO CLUE WHO KIDNAPPED HER.
SORRY!
GOOD MORNING, ERICA!
KILALA, YOU'RE LATE!
Not that that it matters!
AS LONG AS EVERYONE IS HAPPY AND SAFE!
SORRY!
I HAD TO FEED THE PAIR OF FREE-LOADERS.

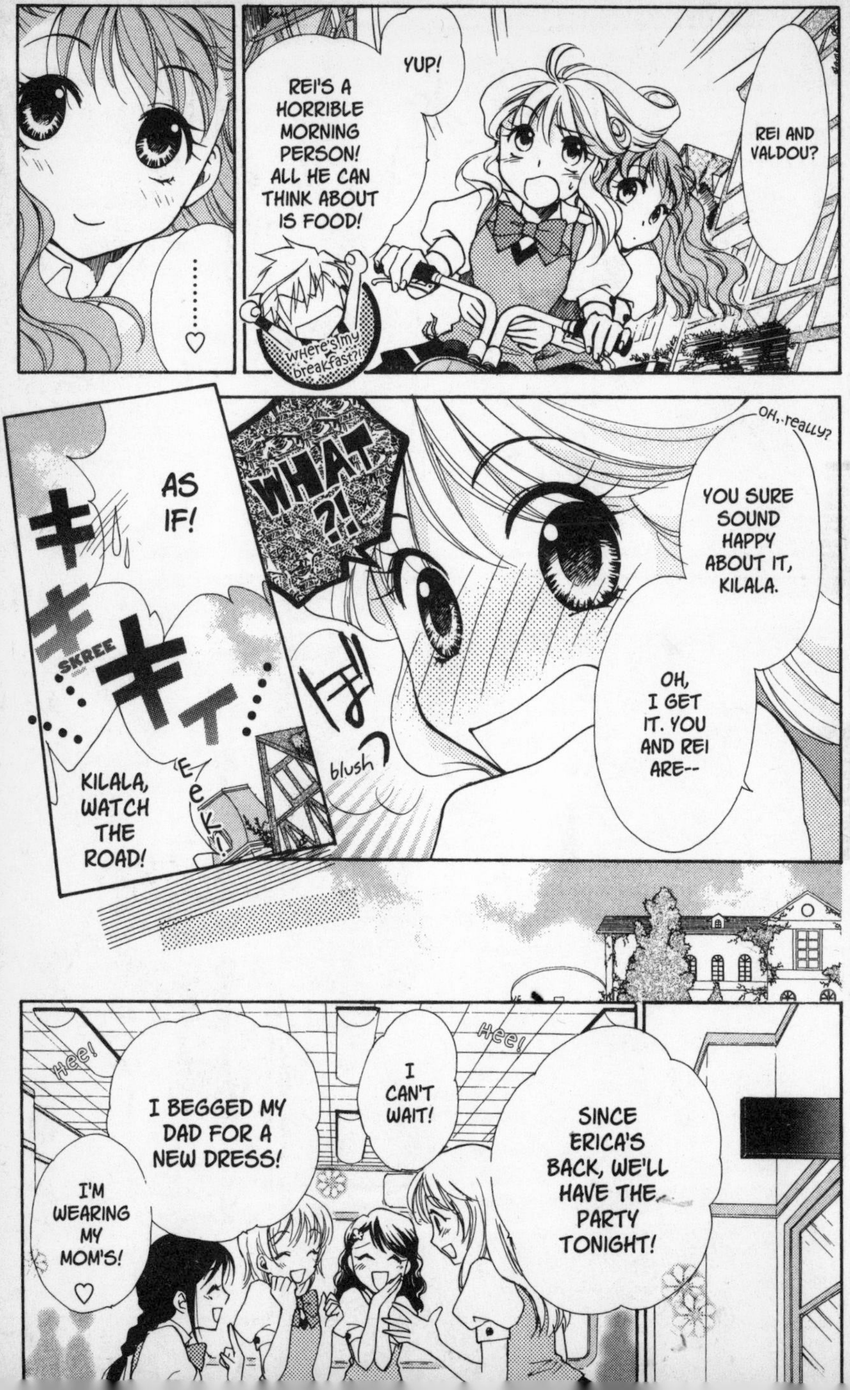
REI AND VALDOU?
YUP!
REI'S A HORRIBLE MORNING PERSON! ALL HE CAN THINK ABOUT IS FOOD!
Where's my breakfast?!
......♡
OH, really?
YOU SURE SOUND HAPPY ABOUT IT, KILALA.
OH, I GET IT. YOU AND REI ARE--
WHAT?!
blush
AS IF!
SKREE
KILALA, WATCH THE ROAD!
Eeek!
SINCE ERICA'S BACK, WE'LL HAVE THE PARTY TONIGHT!
Hee!
I CAN'T WAIT!
I BEGGED MY DAD FOR A NEW DRESS!
Hee!
I'M WEARING MY MOM'S! ♡

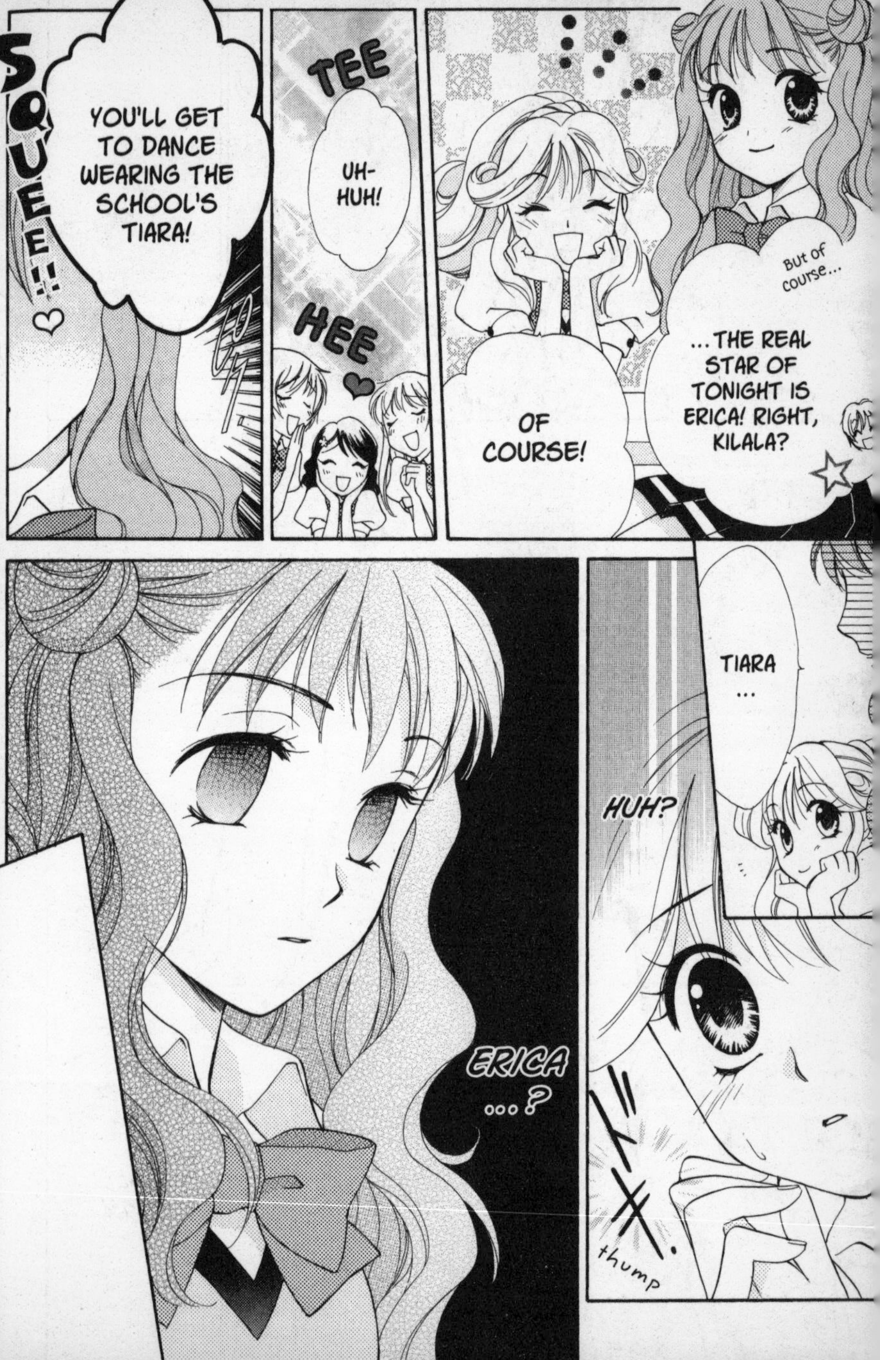
But of course...
...THE REAL STAR OF TONIGHT IS ERICA! RIGHT, KILALA?
OF COURSE!
TEE
UH-HUH!
HEE
YOU'LL GET TO DANCE WEARING THE SCHOOL'S TIARA!
SQUEE!!
TIARA ...
HUH?
thump
ERICA ...?

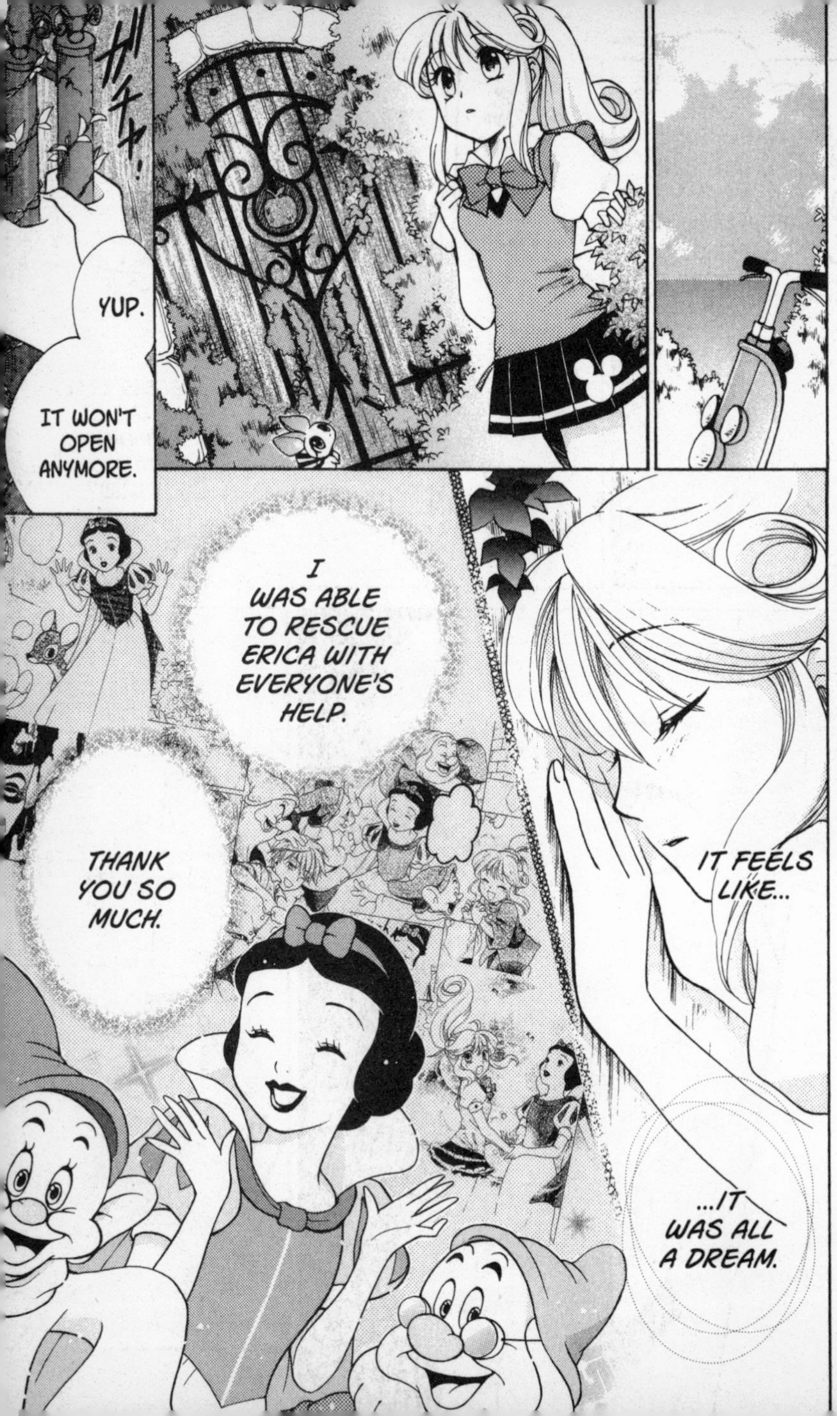
ガチャ!
YUP.
IT WON'T OPEN ANYMORE.
IT FEELS LIKE...
...IT WAS ALL A DREAM.
I WAS ABLE TO RESCUE ERICA WITH EVERYONE'S HELP.
THANK YOU SO MUCH.

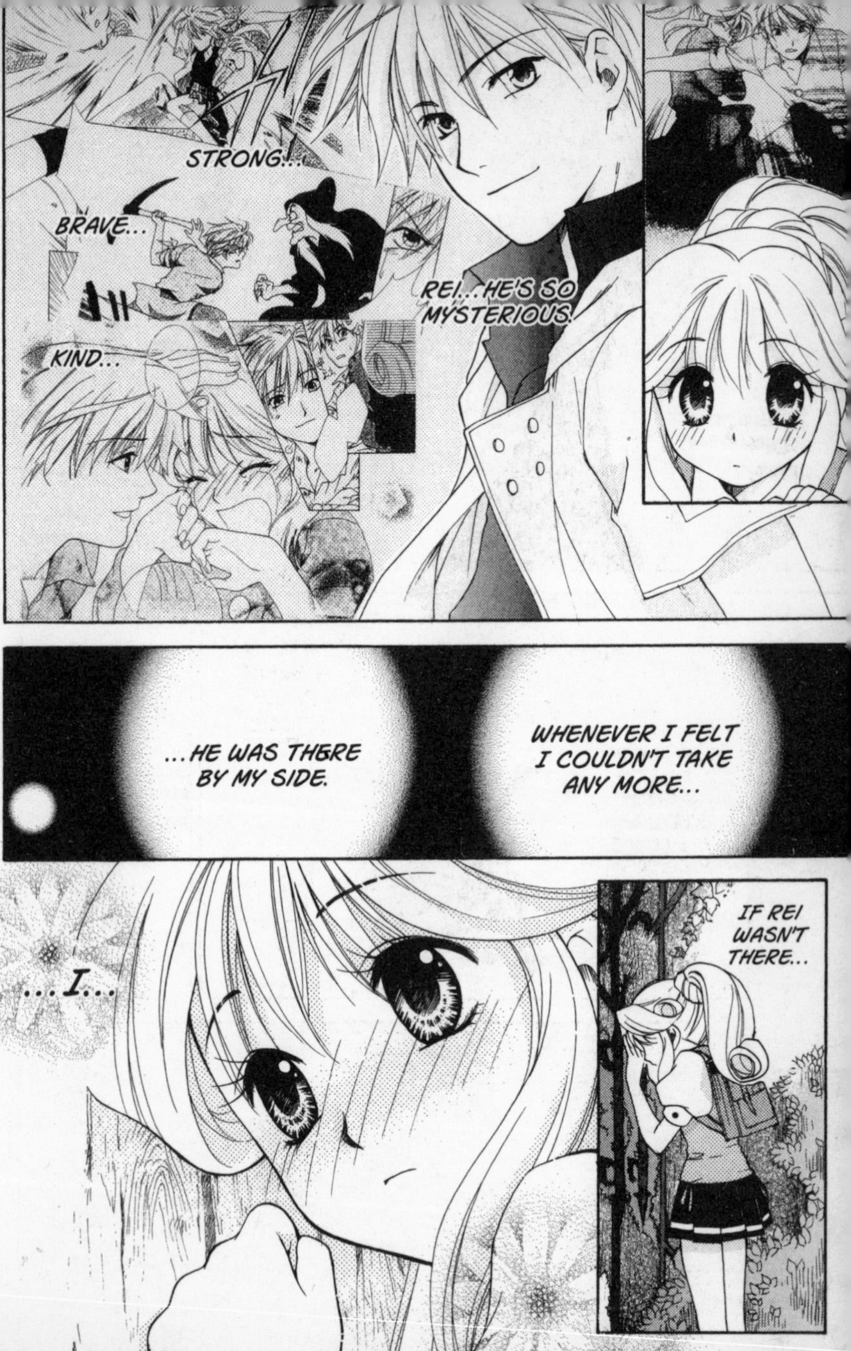
REI...HE'S SO MYSTERIOUS.
STRONG...
BRAVE...
KIND...
WHENEVER I FELT I COULDN'T TAKE ANY MORE...
...HE WAS THERE BY MY SIDE.
IF REI WASN'T THERE...
...I...

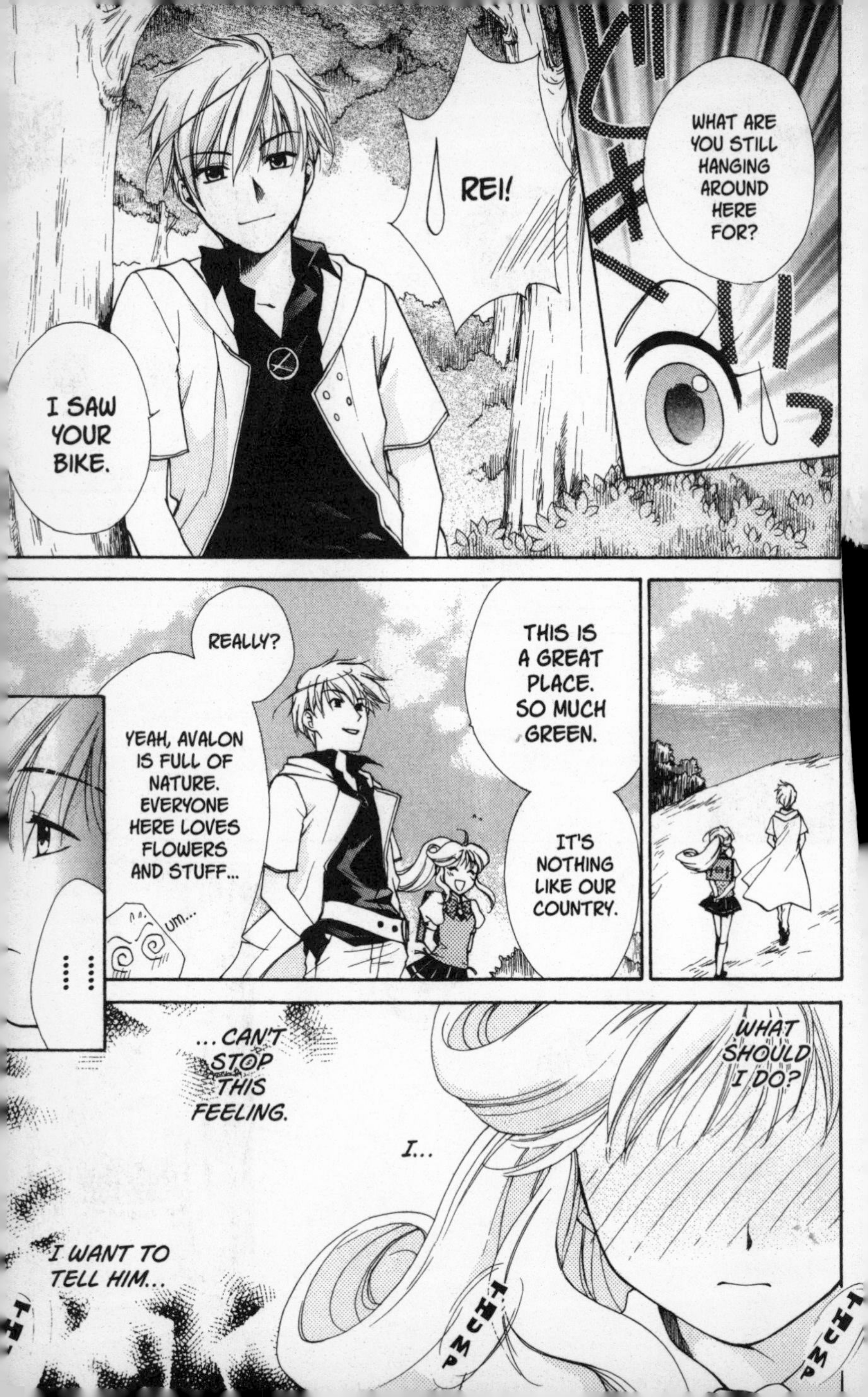
WHAT ARE YOU STILL HANGING AROUND HERE FOR?
REI!
I SAW YOUR BIKE.
THIS IS A GREAT PLACE. SO MUCH GREEN.
IT'S NOTHING LIKE OUR COUNTRY.
REALLY?
YEAH, AVALON IS FULL OF NATURE. EVERYONE HERE LOVES FLOWERS AND STUFF...
UM...
......
WHAT SHOULD I DO?
THUMP
I...
...CAN'T STOP THIS FEELING.
THUMP
I WANT TO TELL HIM...

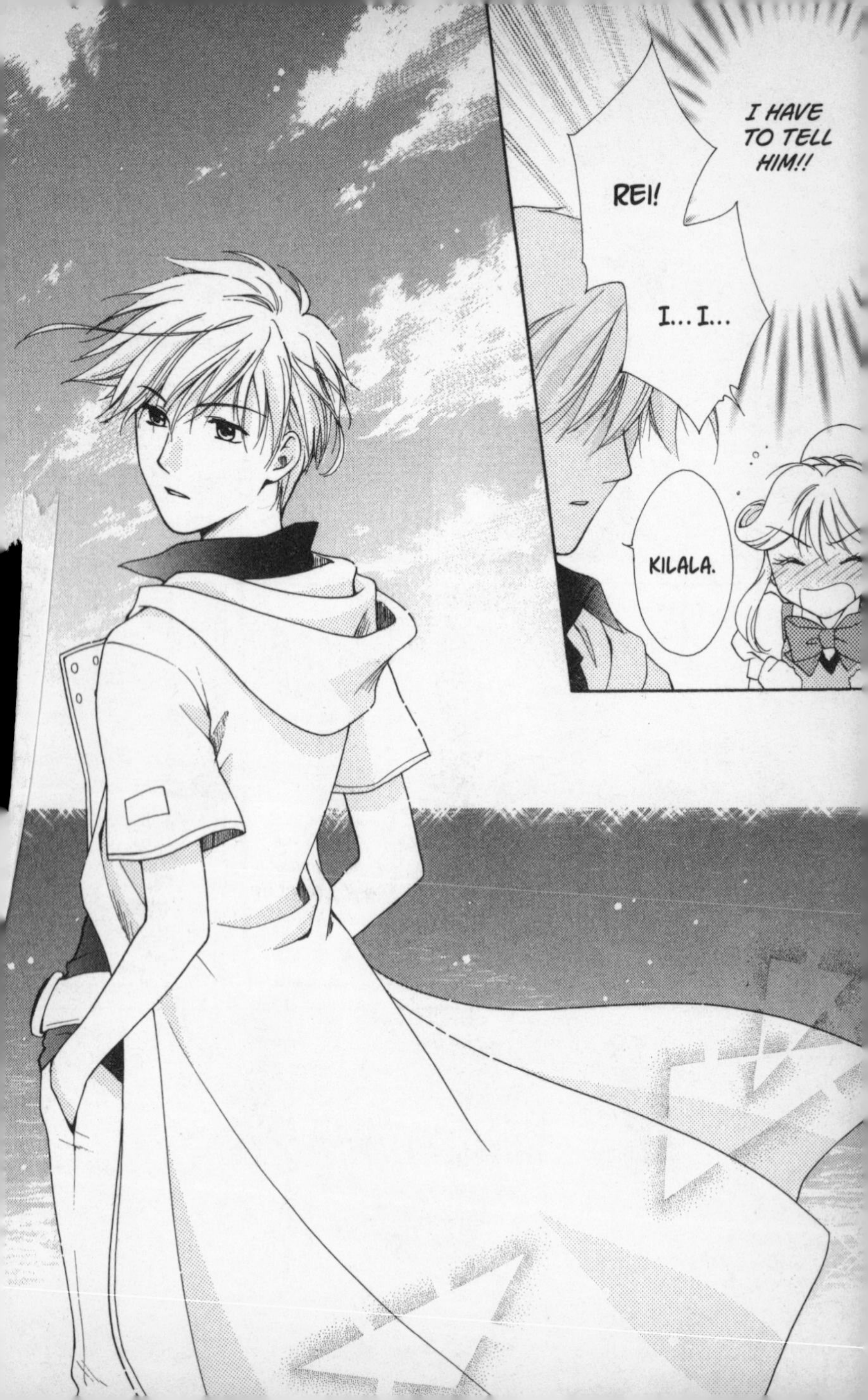
I HAVE TO TELL HIM!!
REI!
I... I...
KILALA.

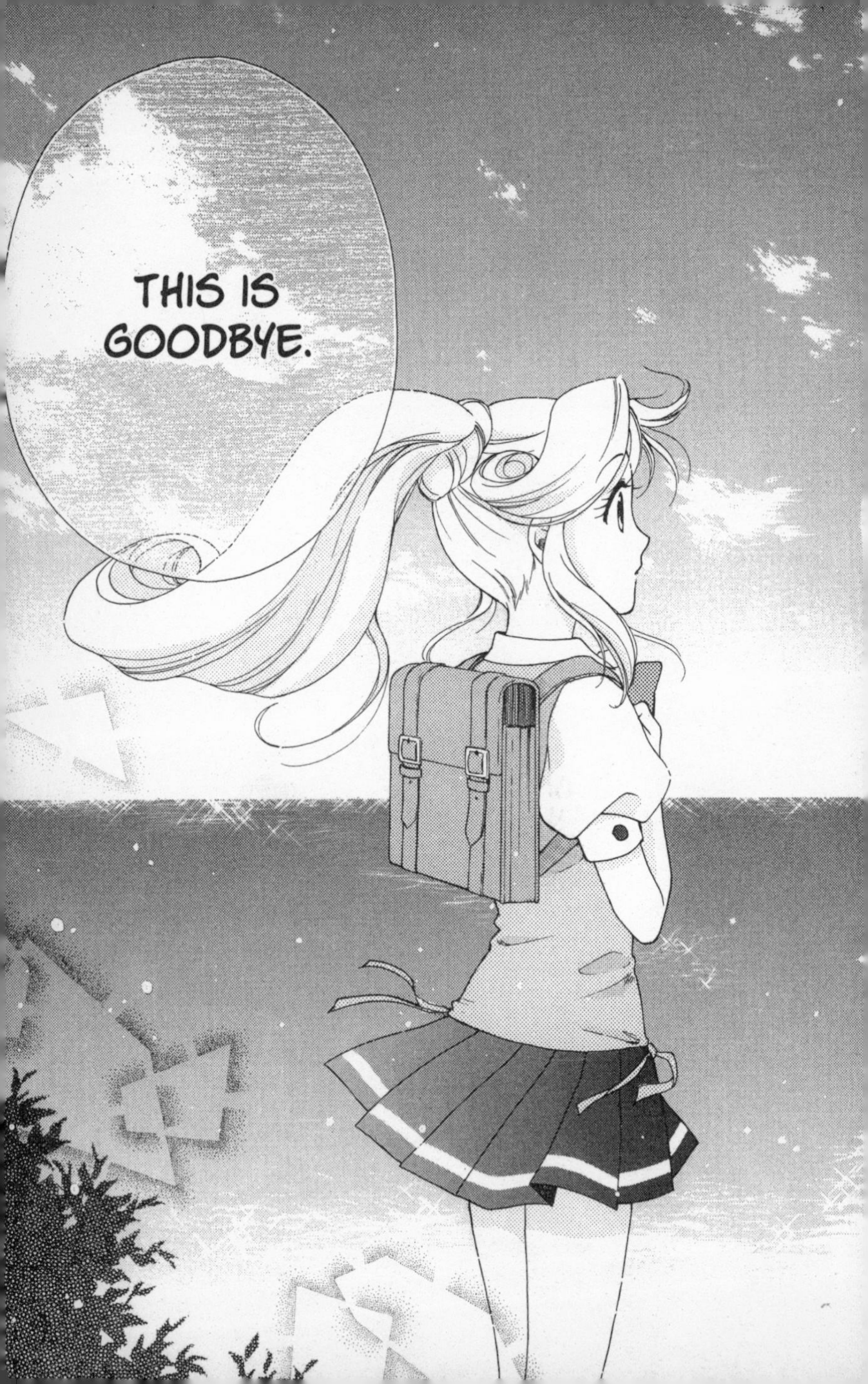
THIS IS GOODBYE.

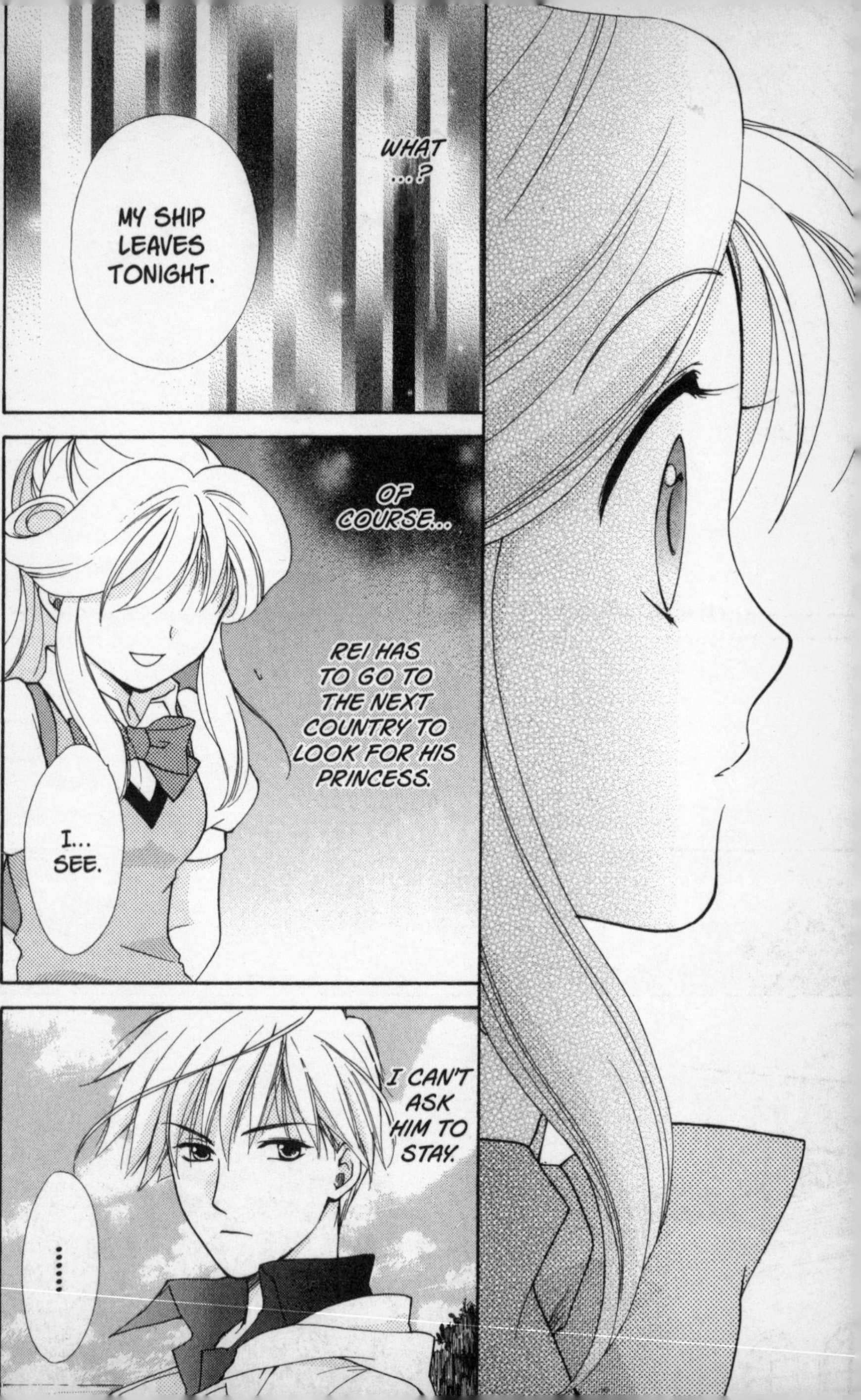
WHAT ...?
MY SHIP LEAVES TONIGHT.
OF COURSE...
REI HAS TO GO TO THE NEXT COUNTRY TO LOOK FOR HIS PRINCESS.
I... SEE.
I CAN'T ASK HIM TO STAY.
......

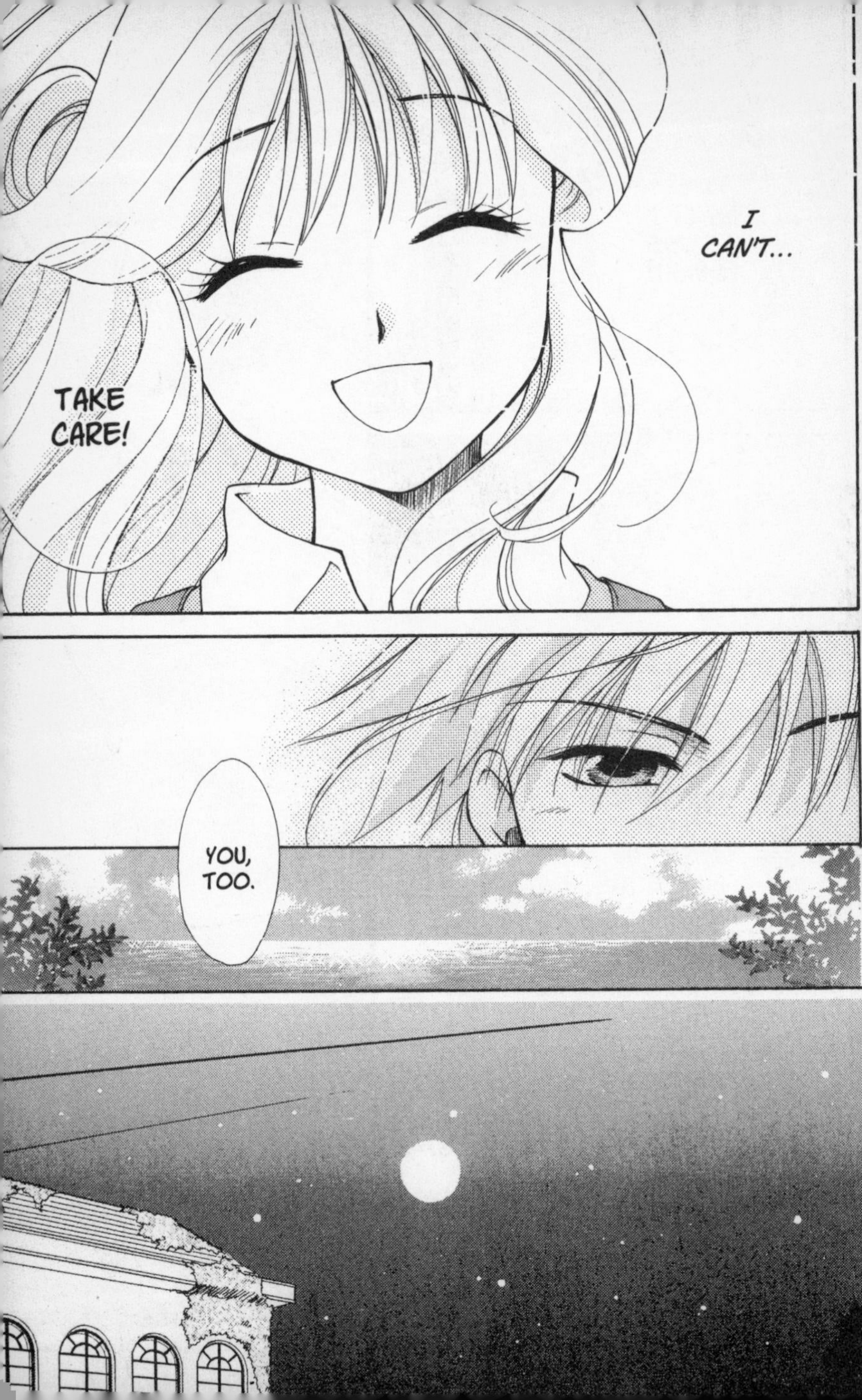

I CAN'T...
TAKE CARE!
YOU, TOO.

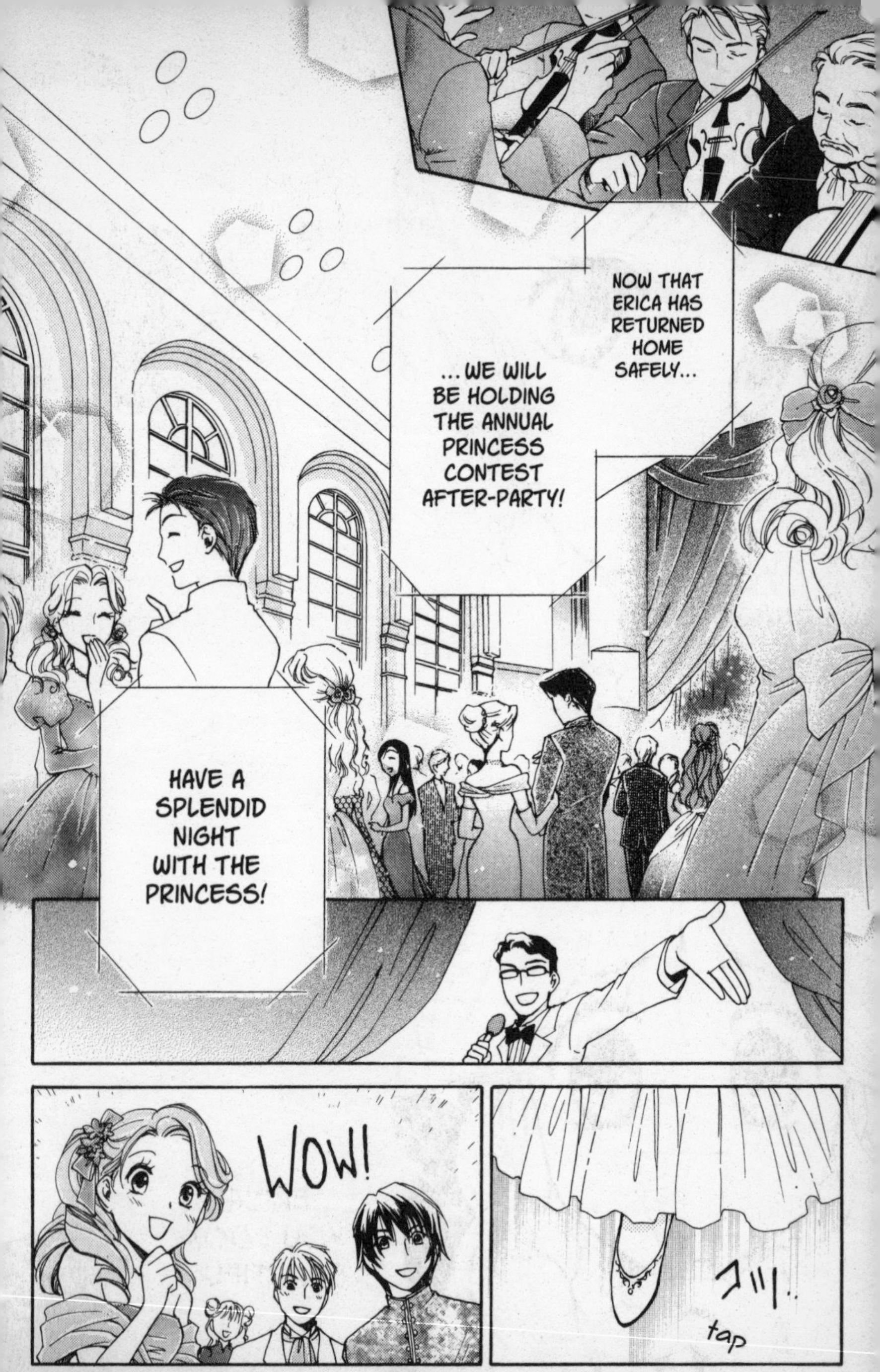
NOW THAT ERICA HAS RETURNED HOME SAFELY...
...WE WILL BE HOLDING THE ANNUAL PRINCESS CONTEST AFTER-PARTY!
HAVE A SPLENDID NIGHT WITH THE PRINCESS!
tap
WOW!

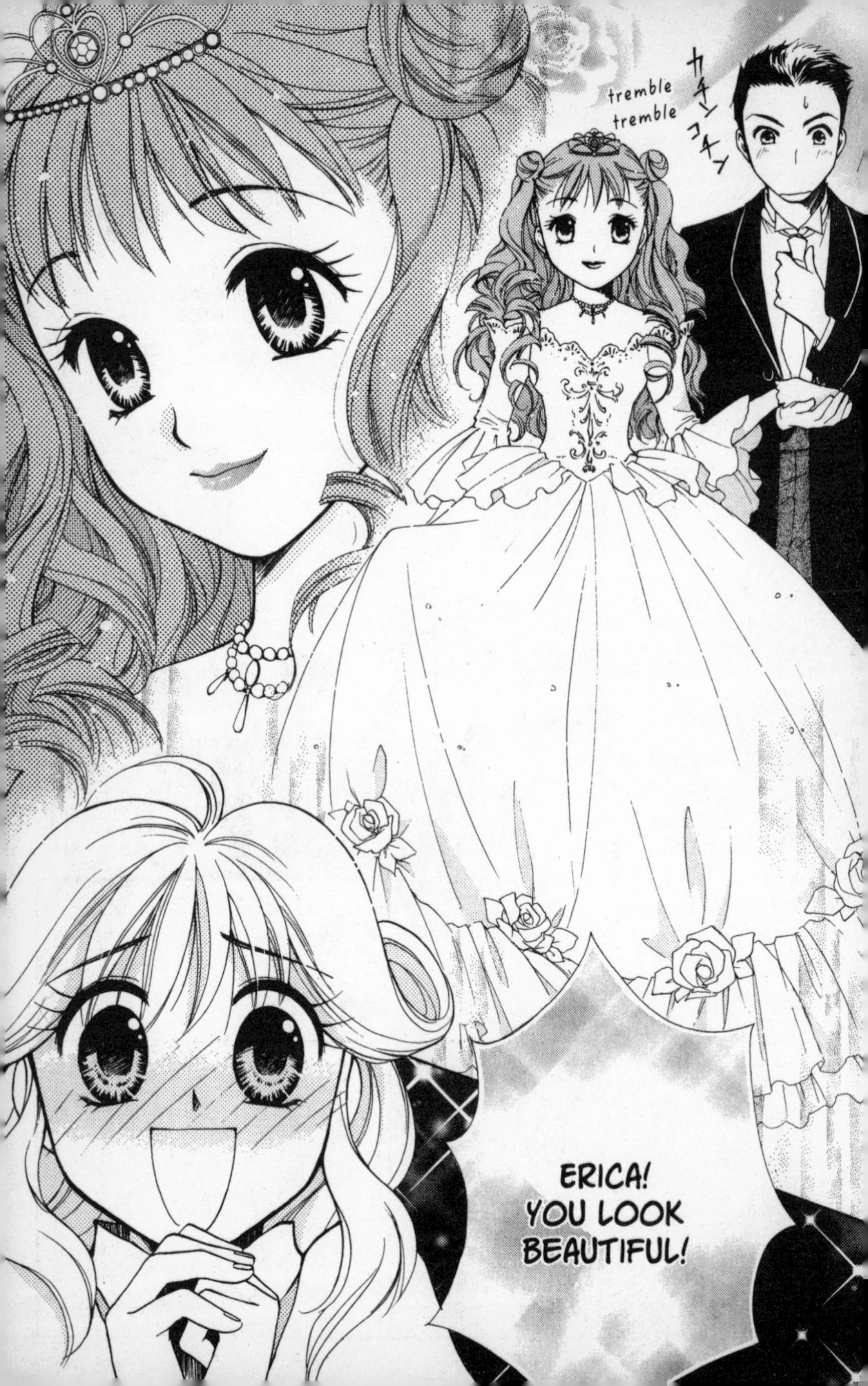
カチンコチン
tremble tremble
ERICA! YOU LOOK BEAUTIFUL!

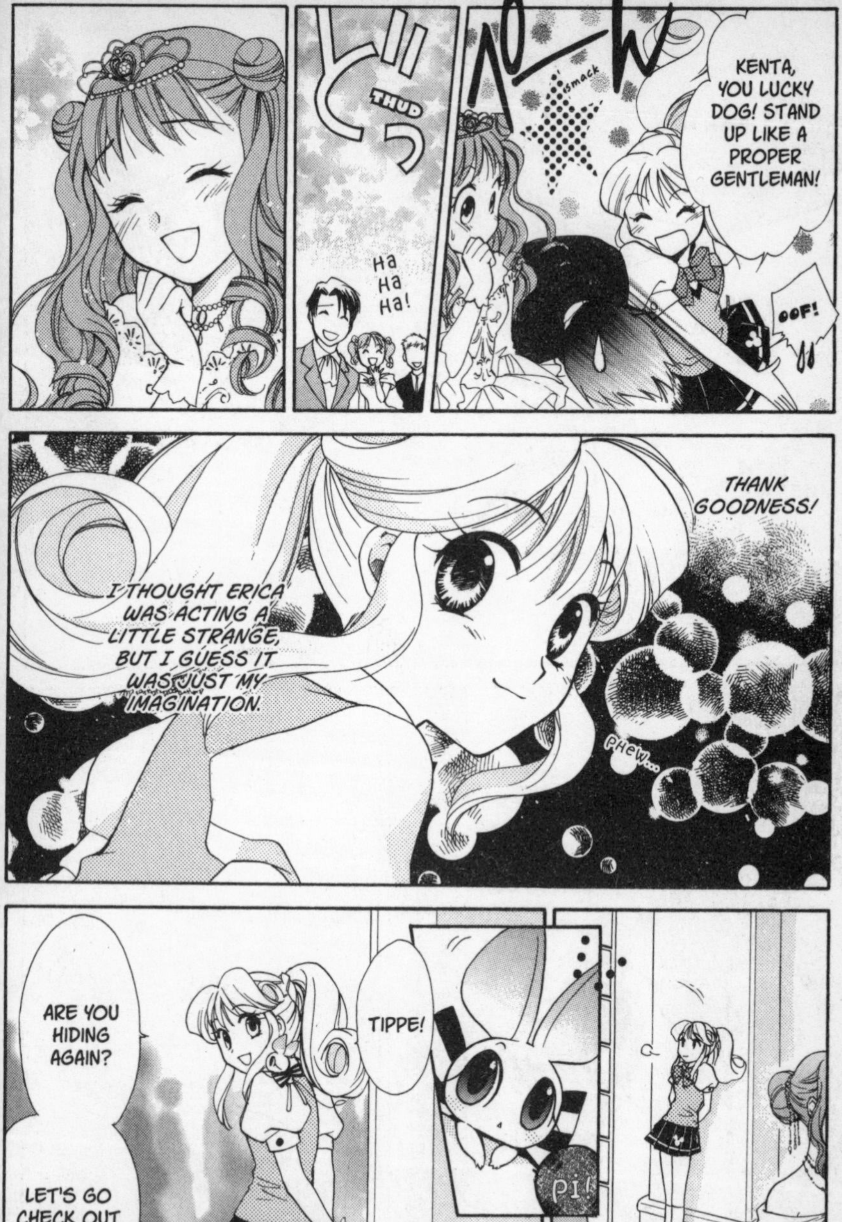
smack
KENTA, YOU LUCKY DOG! STAND UP LIKE A PROPER GENTLEMAN!
OOF!
THUD
HA HA HA!
THANK GOODNESS!
I THOUGHT ERICA WAS ACTING A LITTLE STRANGE, BUT I GUESS IT WAS JUST MY IMAGINATION.
PHEW...
TIPPE!
PI!
ARE YOU HIDING AGAIN?
LET'S GO CHECK OUT THE PARTY.

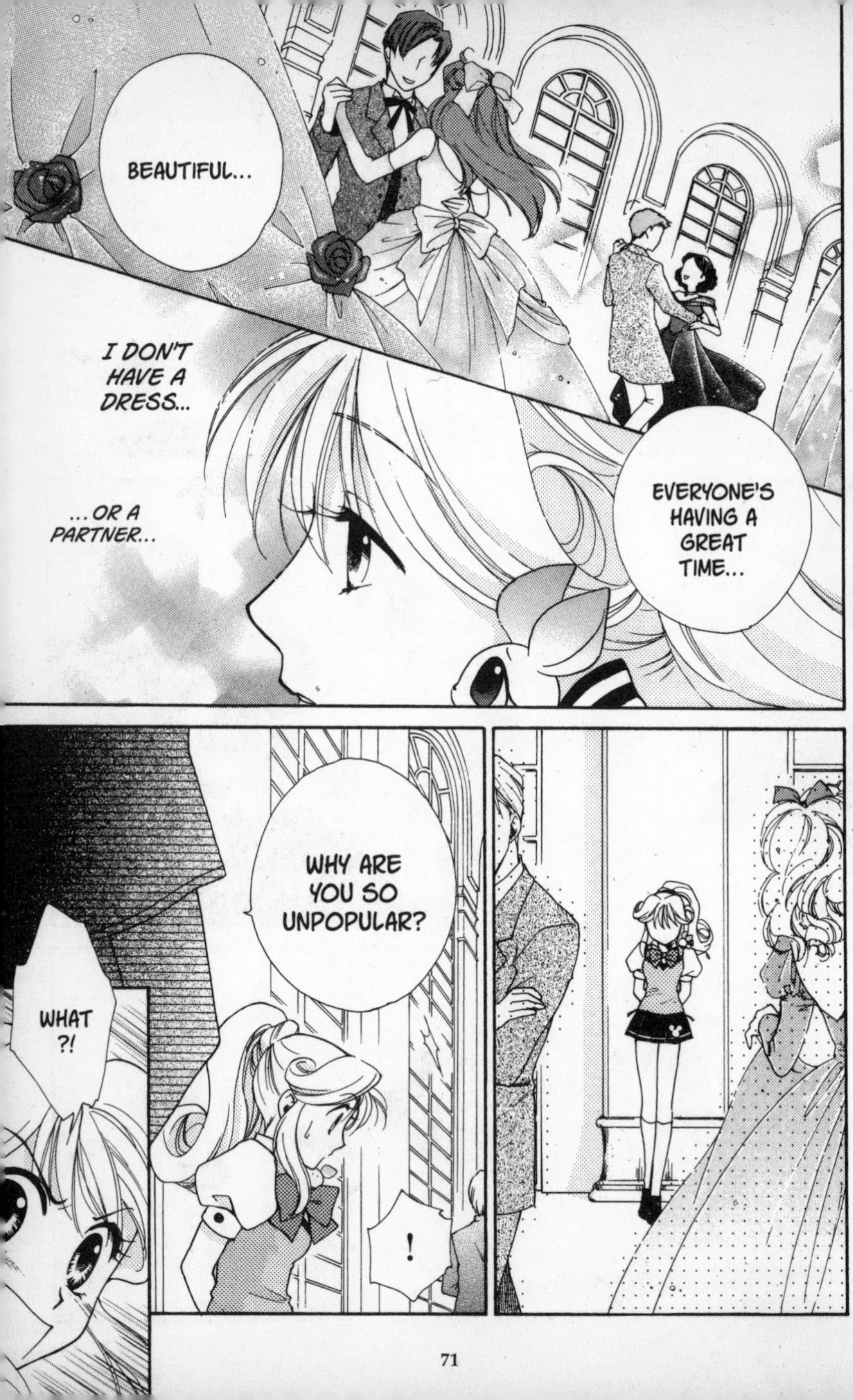
BEAUTIFUL...
EVERYONE'S HAVING A GREAT TIME...
I DON'T HAVE A DRESS...
...OR A PARTNER...
WHY ARE YOU SO UNPOPULAR?
!
WHAT ?!

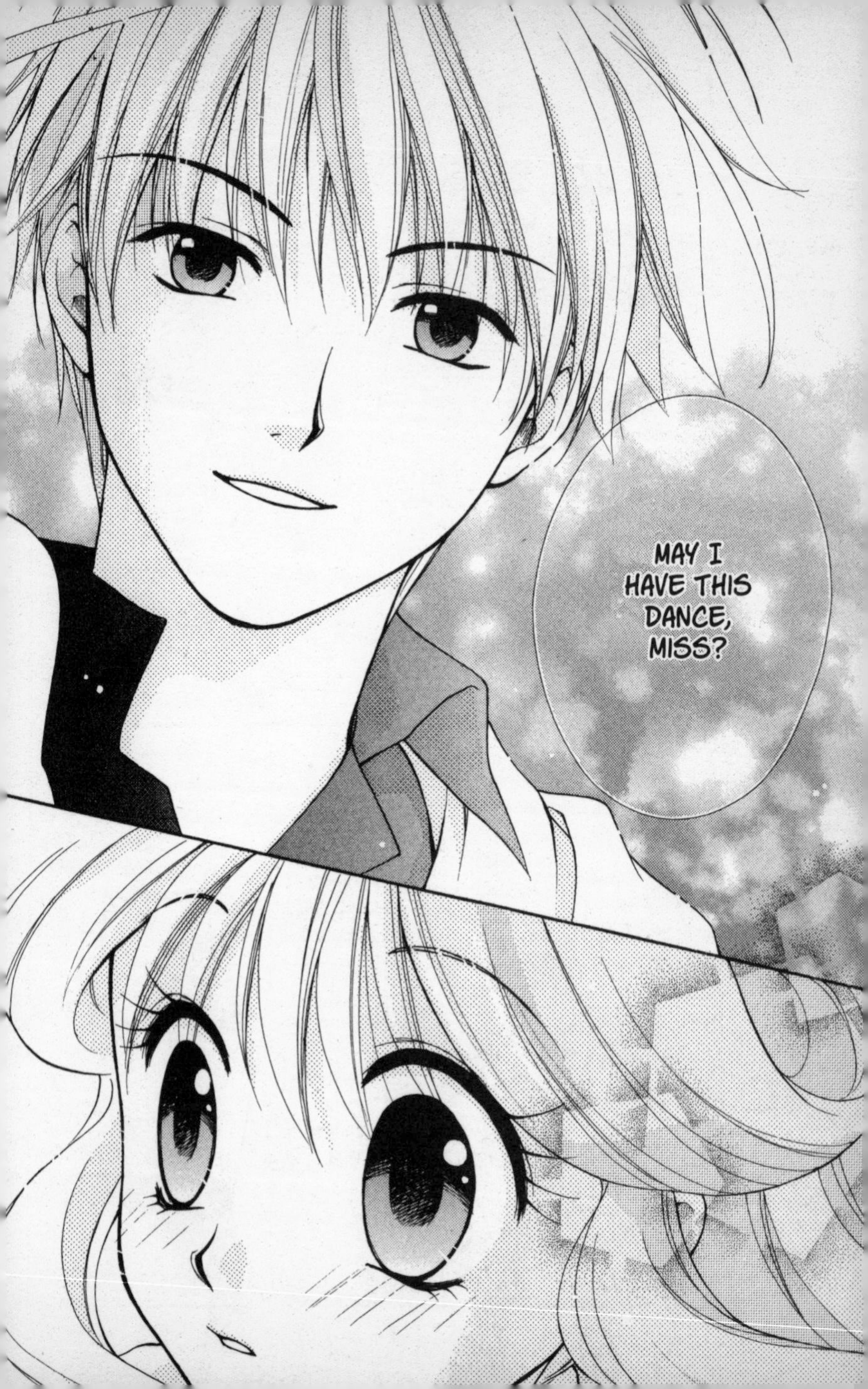
MAY I HAVE THIS DANCE, MISS?

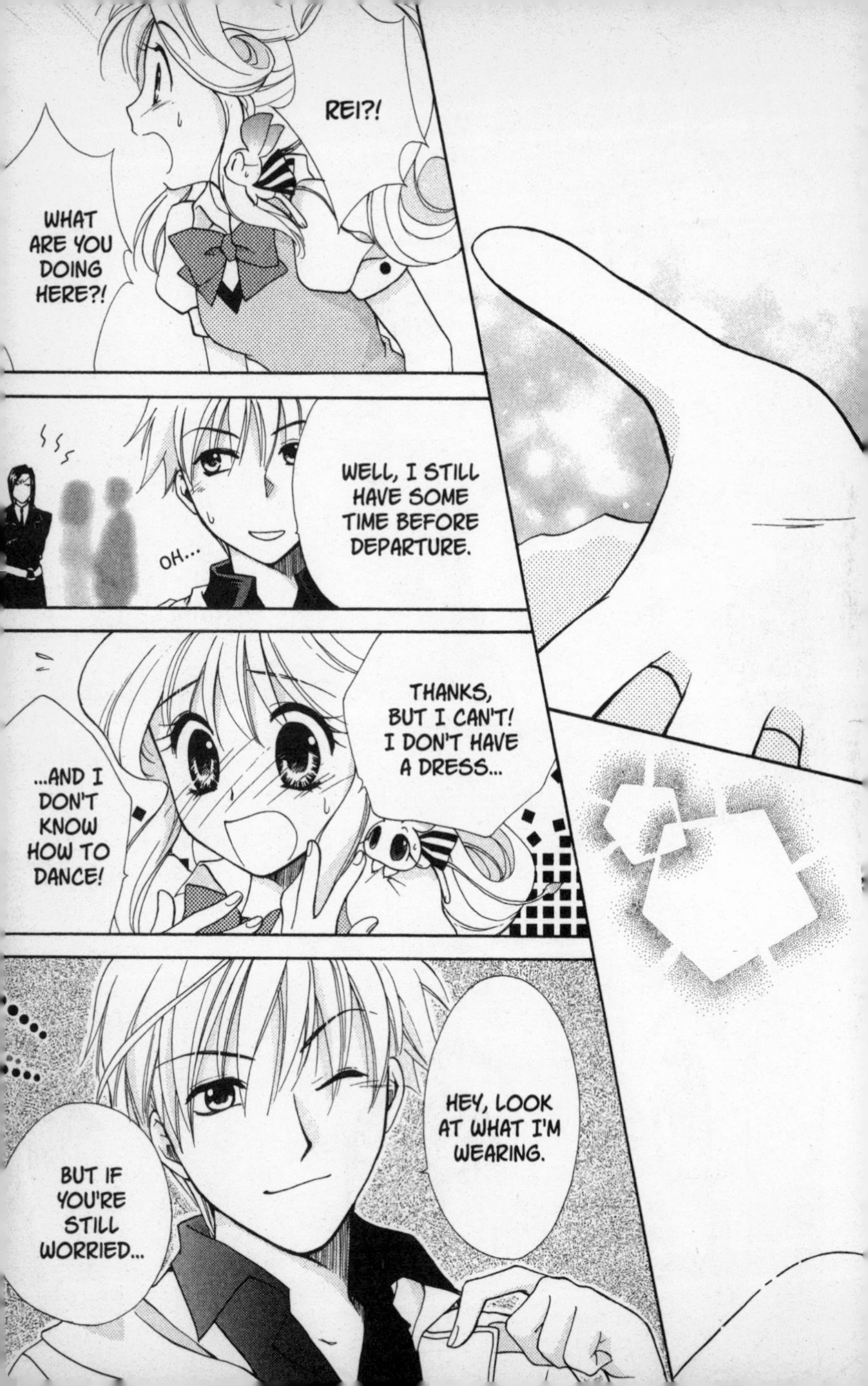
REI?!
WHAT ARE YOU DOING HERE?!
WELL, I STILL HAVE SOME TIME BEFORE DEPARTURE.
OH...
THANKS, BUT I CAN'T! I DON'T HAVE A DRESS...
...AND I DON'T KNOW HOW TO DANCE!
HEY, LOOK AT WHAT I'M WEARING.
BUT IF YOU'RE STILL WORRIED...

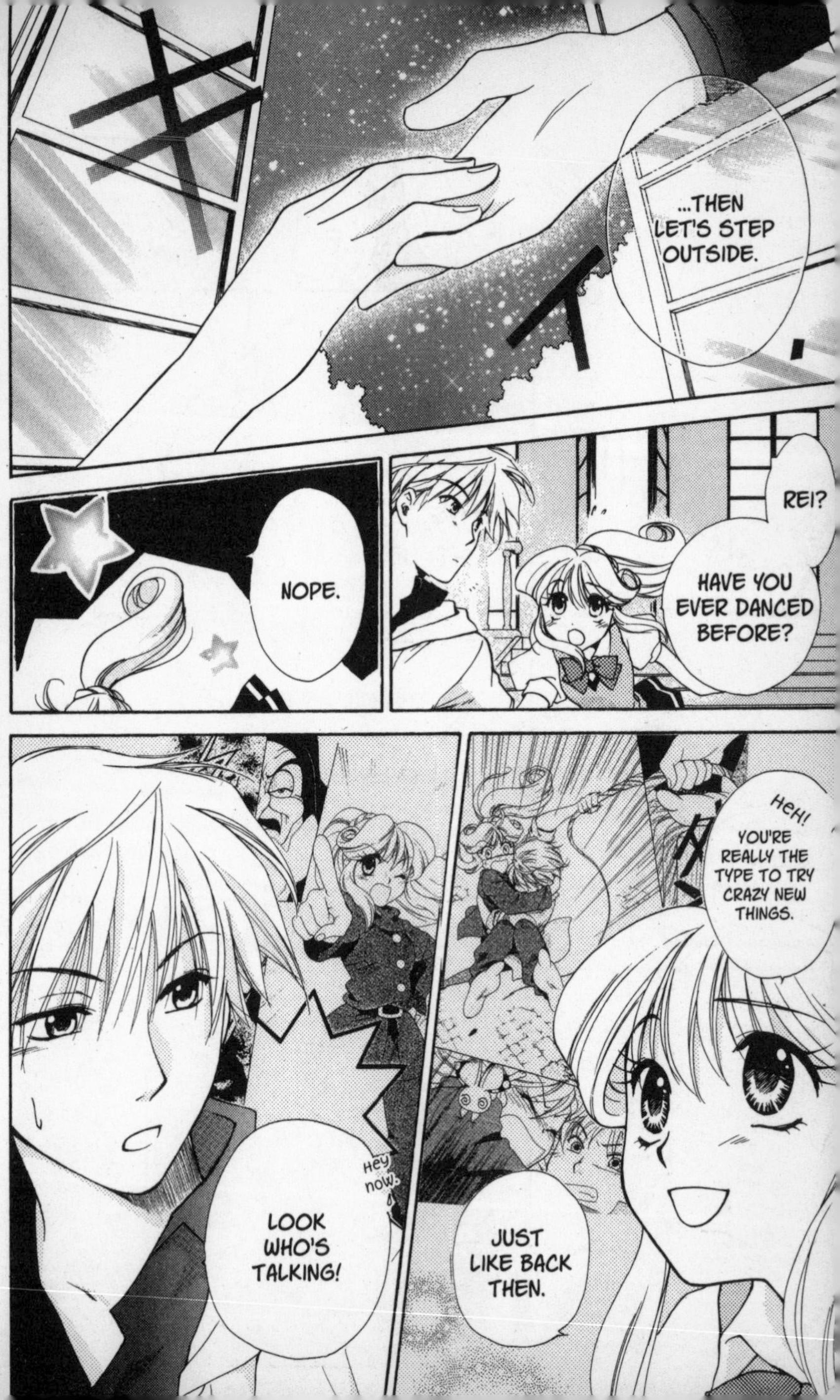
...THEN LET'S STEP OUTSIDE.
REI?
HAVE YOU EVER DANCED BEFORE?
NOPE.
HEH!
YOU'RE REALLY THE TYPE TO TRY CRAZY NEW THINGS.
JUST LIKE BACK THEN.
Hey now.
LOOK WHO'S TALKING!

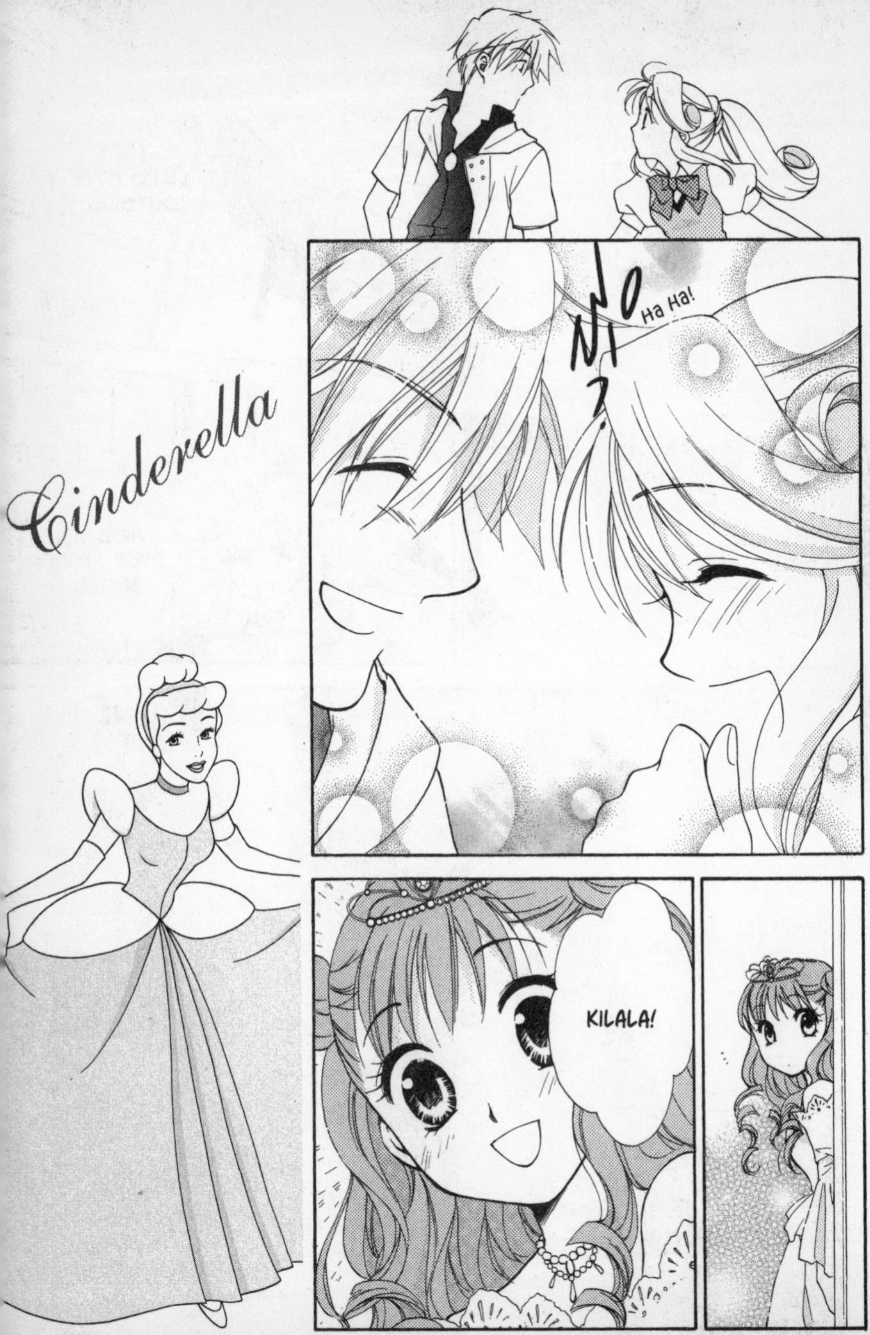
Ha Ha!
Cinderella
KILALA!

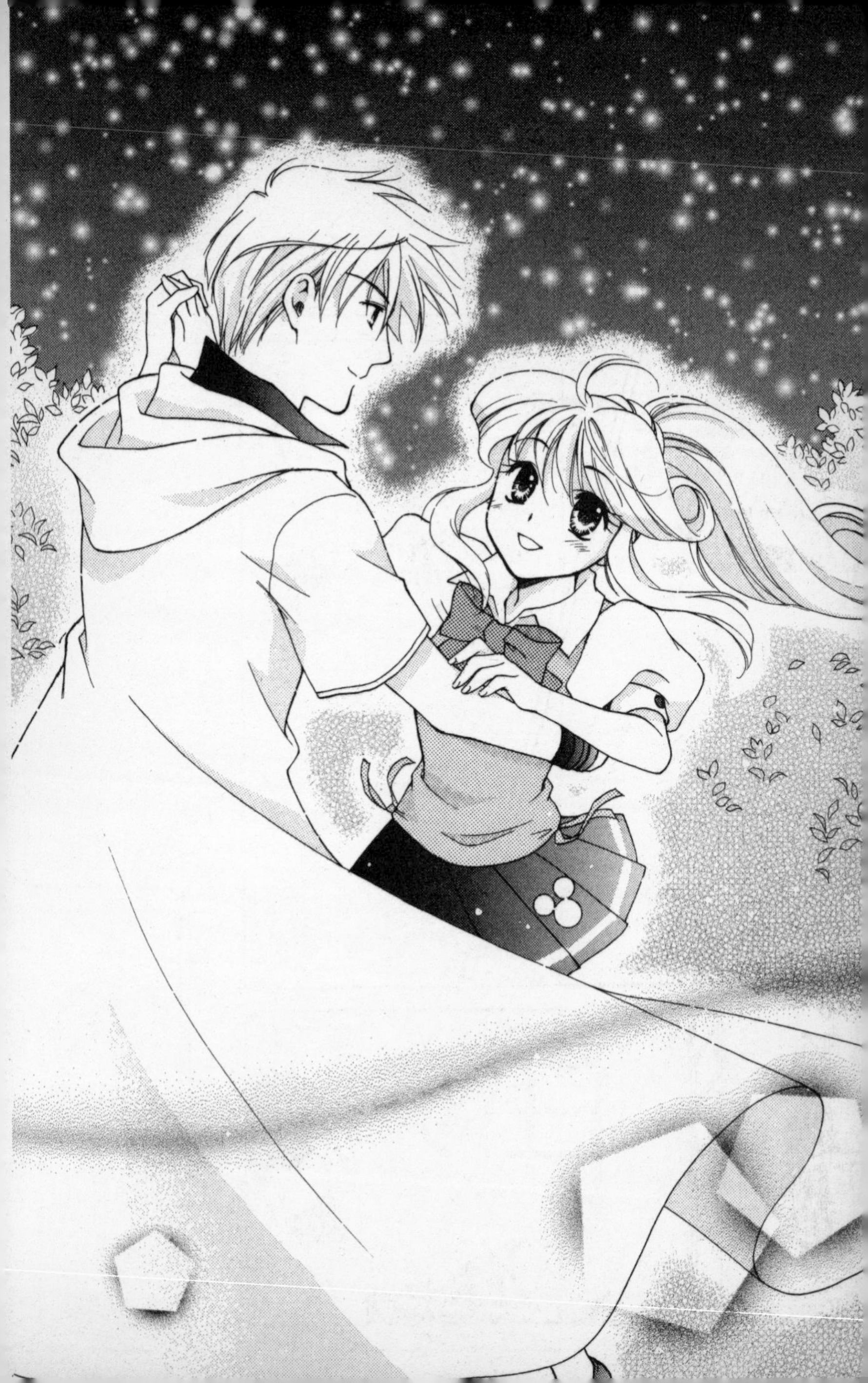

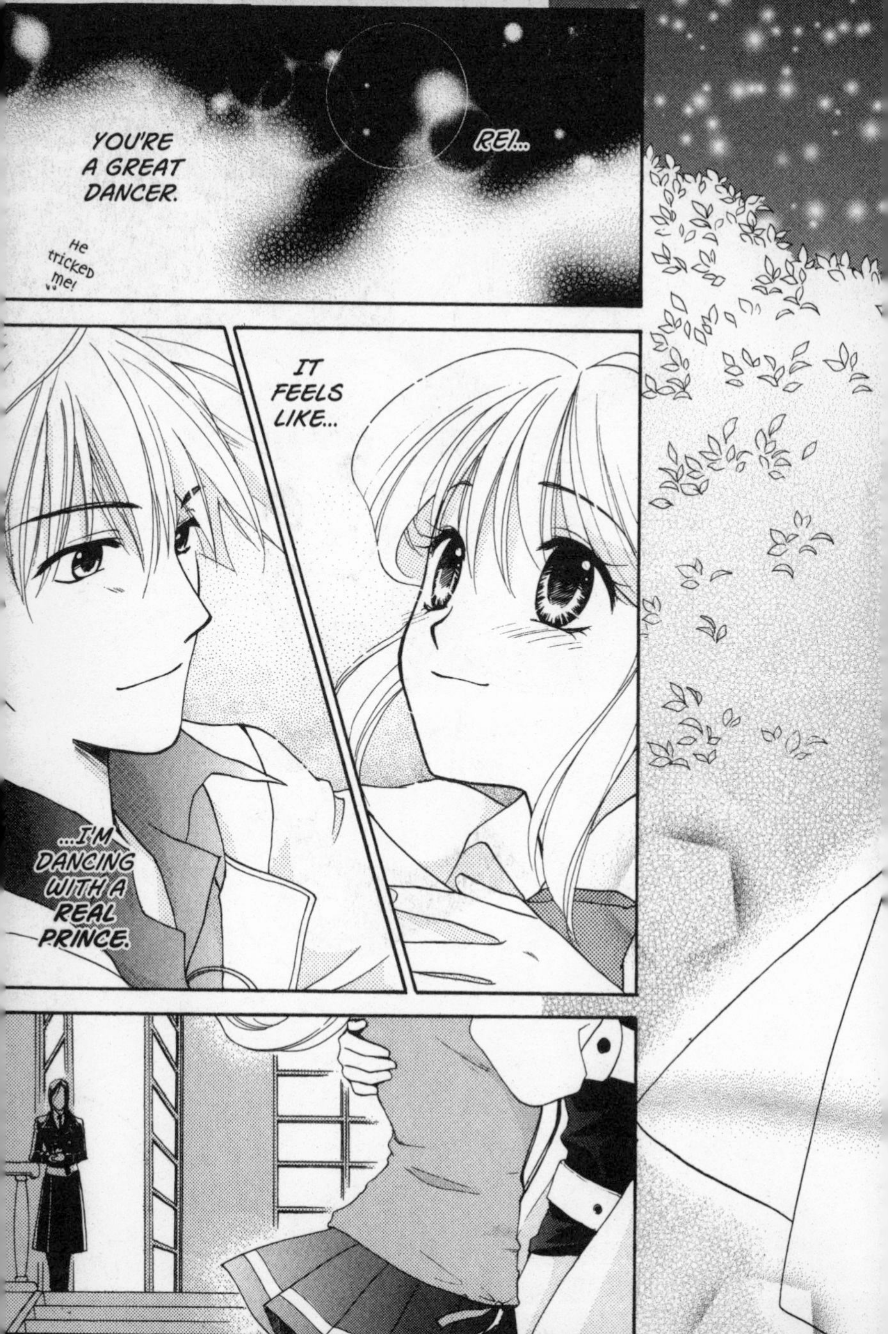
REI...
YOU'RE A GREAT DANCER.
He tricked me!
IT FEELS LIKE...
...I'M DANCING WITH A REAL PRINCE.

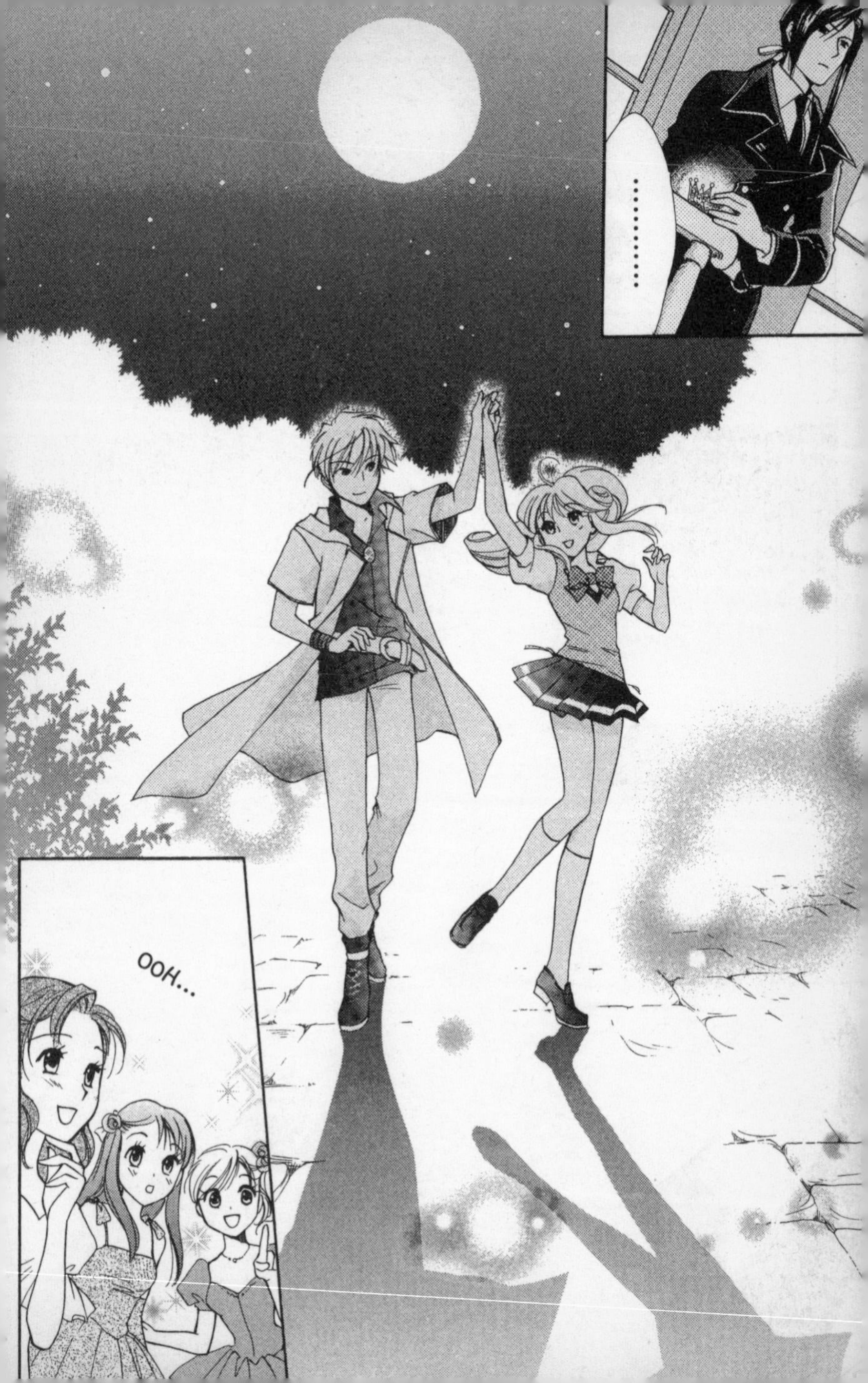
......
OOH...

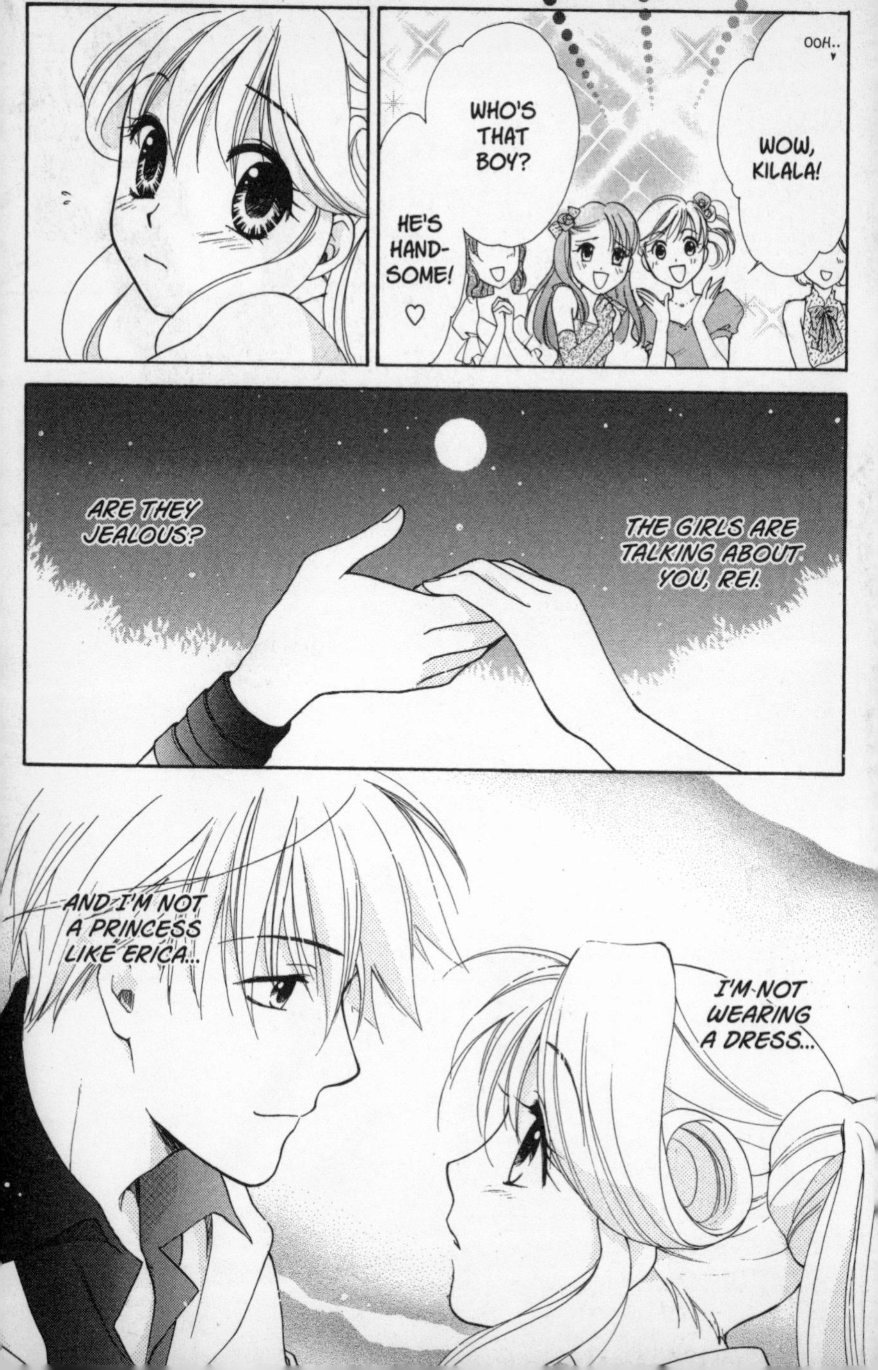
OOH..
WOW, KILALA!
WHO'S THAT BOY?
HE'S HAND-SOME!
THE GIRLS ARE TALKING ABOUT YOU, REI.
ARE THEY JEALOUS?
I'M NOT WEARING A DRESS...
AND I'M NOT A PRINCESS LIKE ERICA...

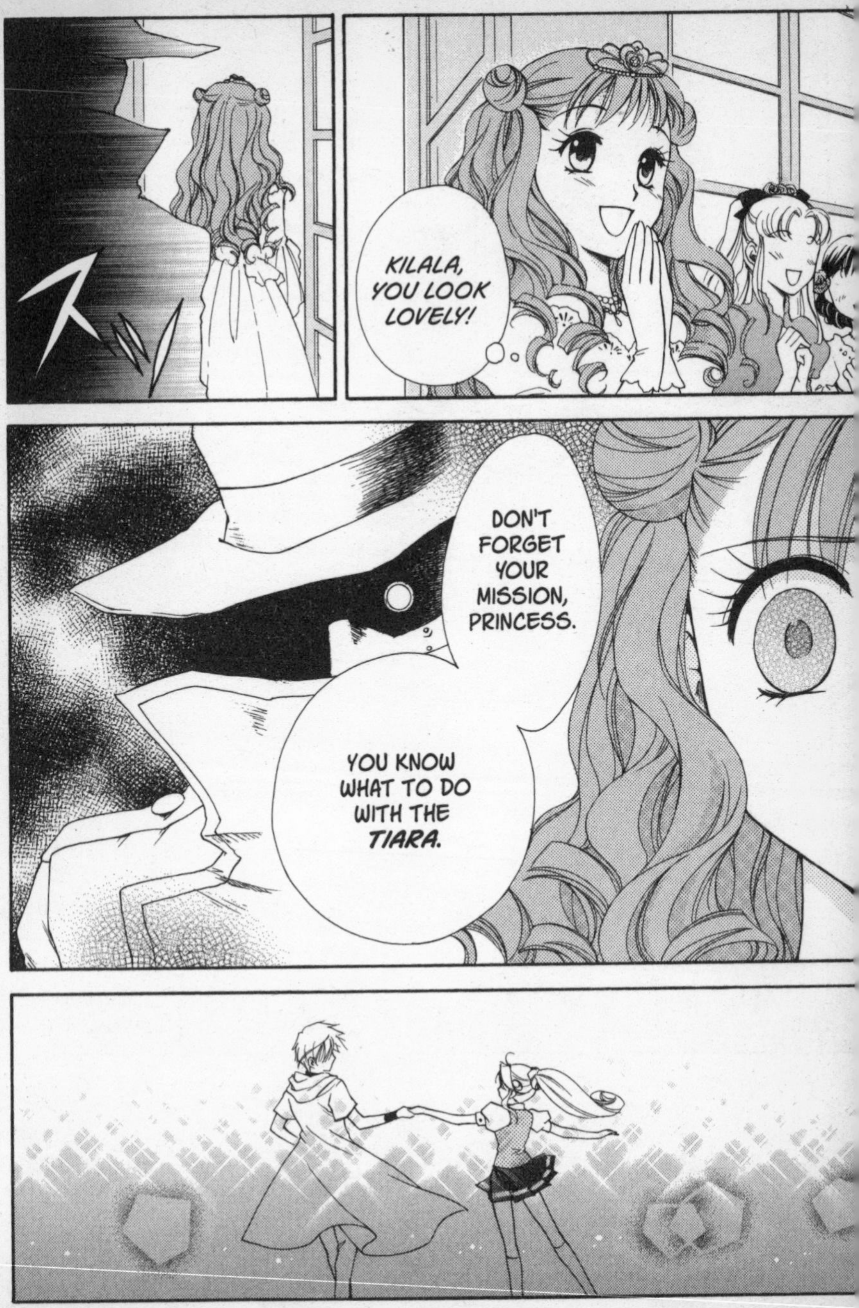
KILALA, YOU LOOK LOVELY!
DON'T FORGET YOUR MISSION, PRINCESS.
YOU KNOW WHAT TO DO WITH THE *TIARA*.

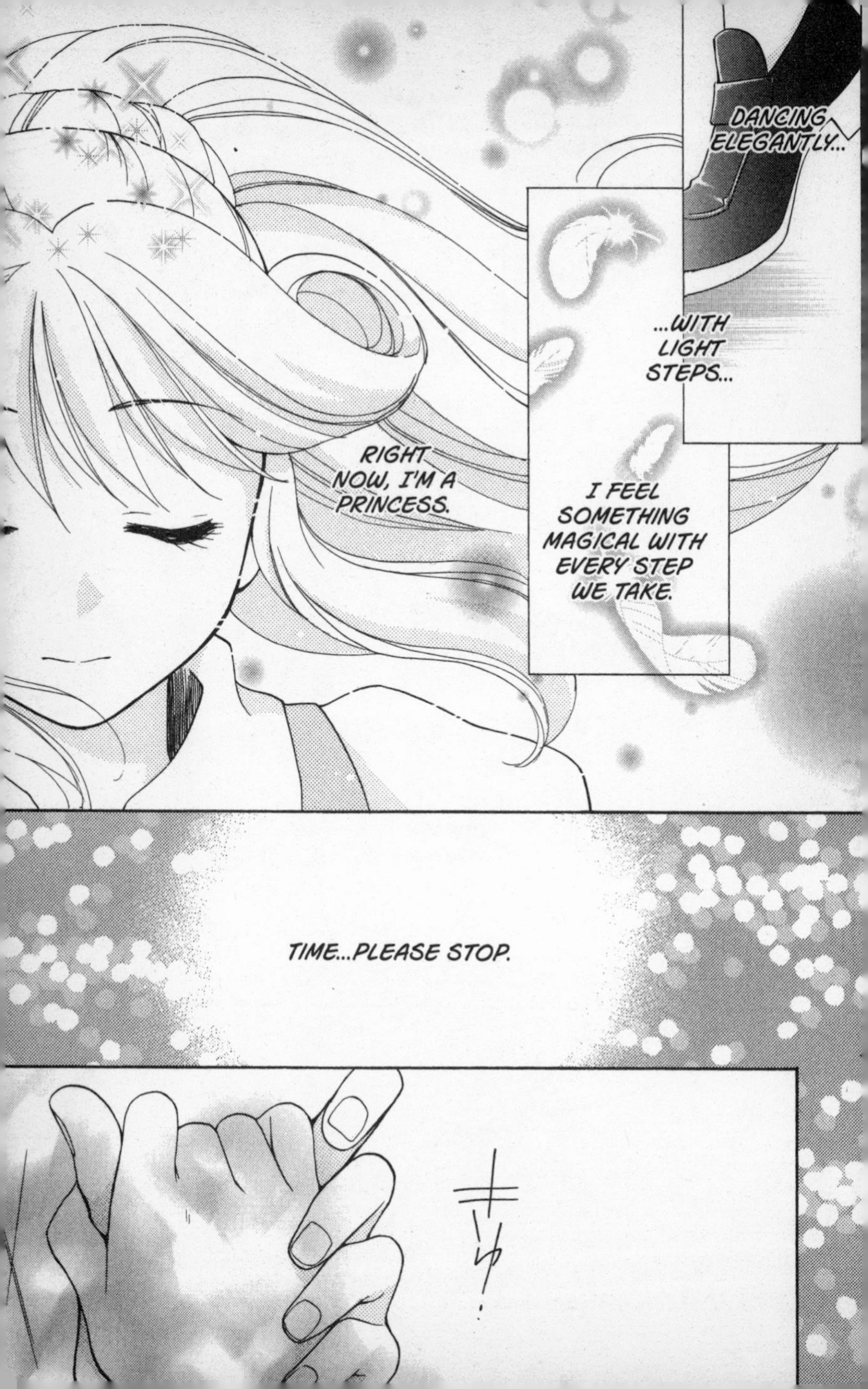
DANCING ELEGANTLY...
...WITH LIGHT STEPS...
I FEEL SOMETHING MAGICAL WITH EVERY STEP WE TAKE.
RIGHT NOW, I'M A PRINCESS.
TIME...PLEASE STOP.
キゅ!

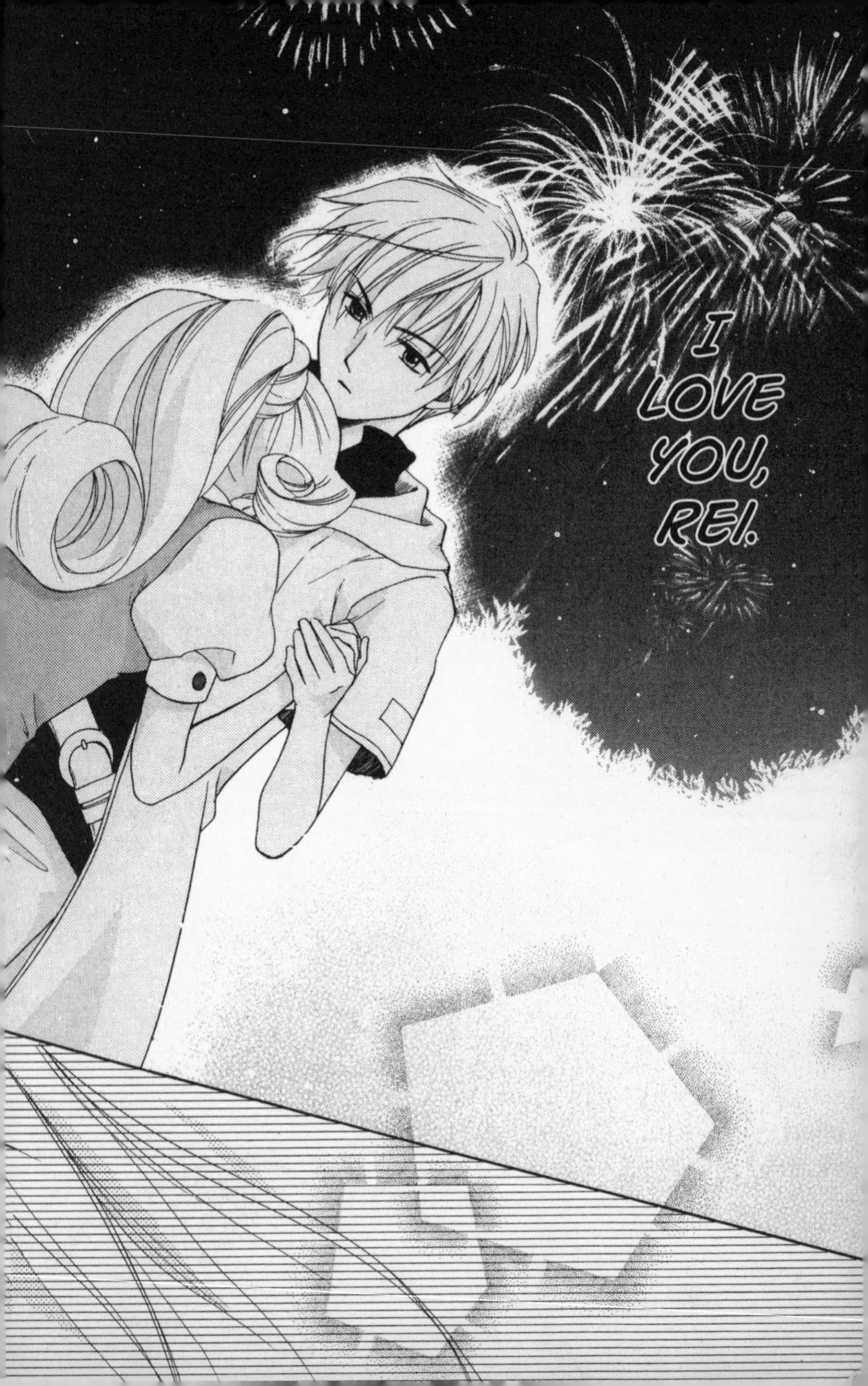
I LOVE YOU, REI.

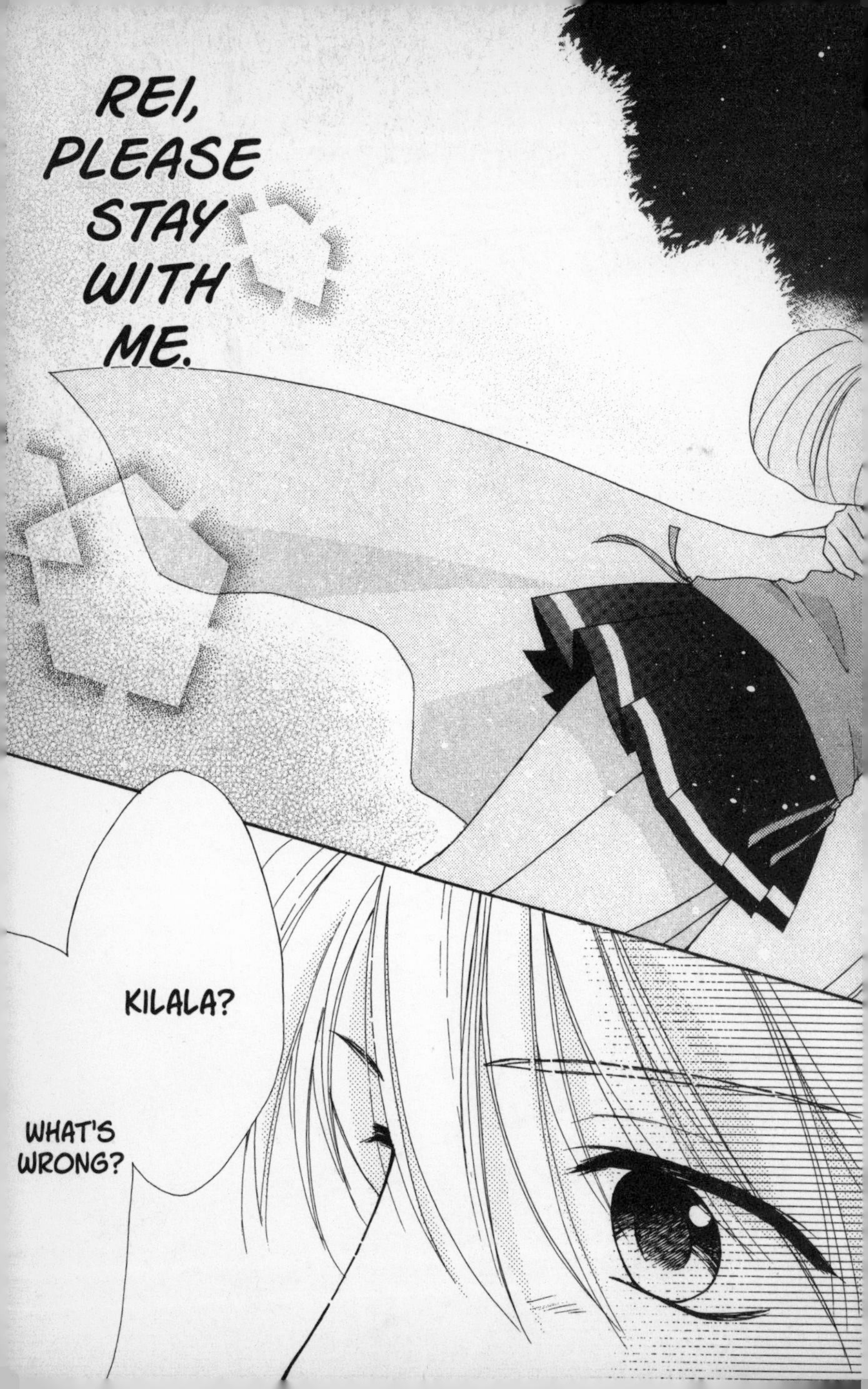
REI, PLEASE STAY WITH ME.
KILALA?
WHAT'S WRONG?

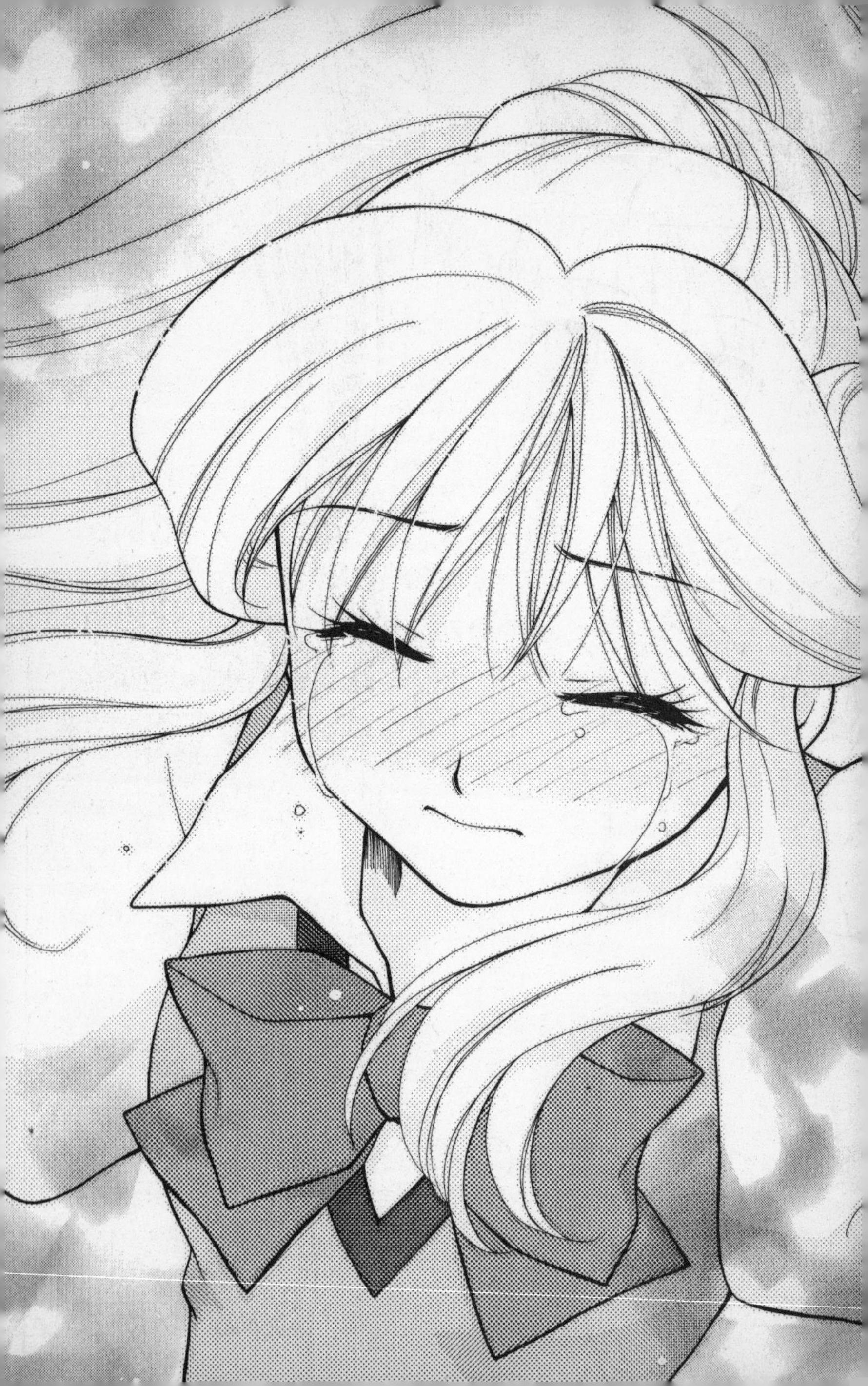

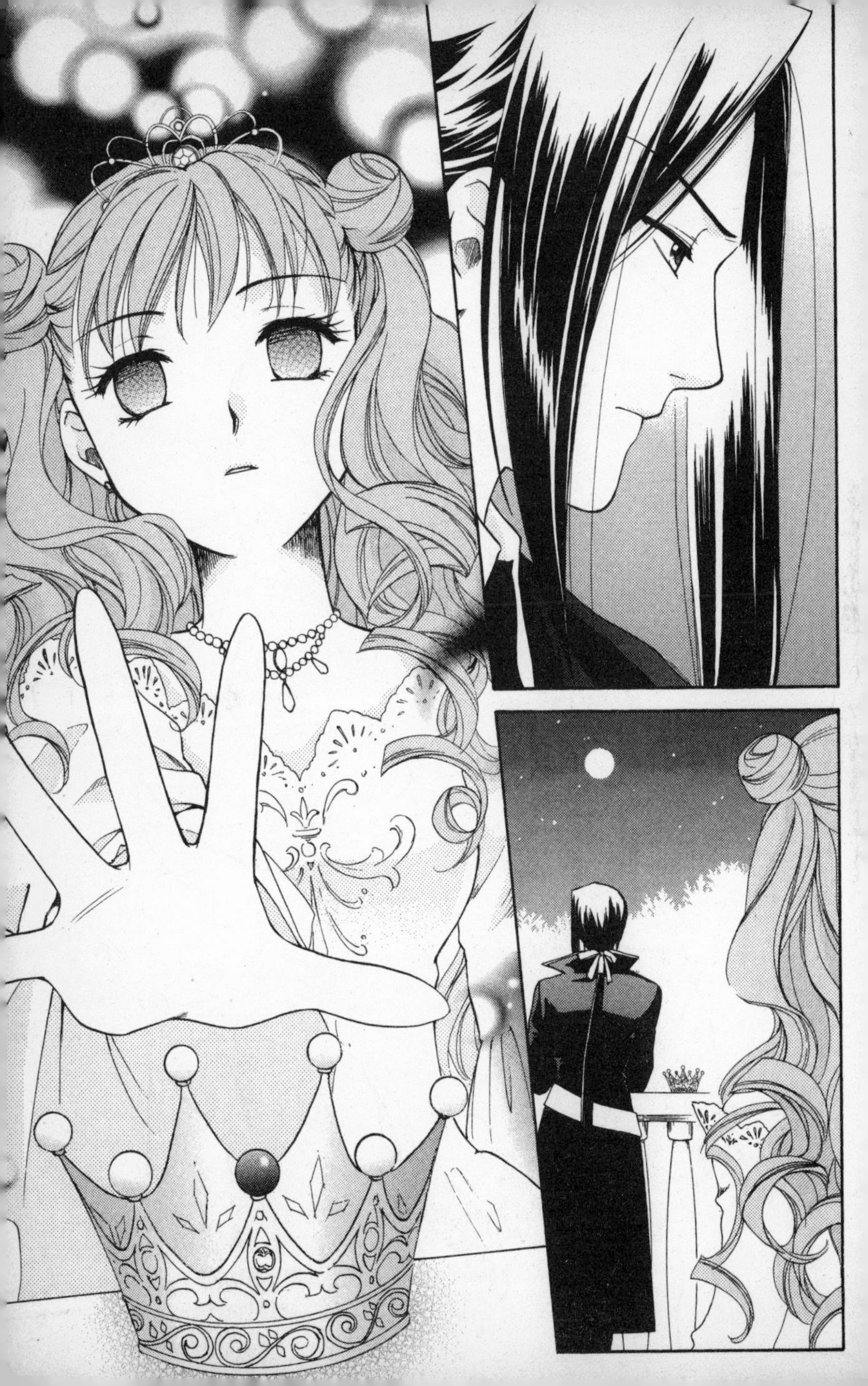

IN THE NEXT VOLUME OF

Disney's
Kilala Princess

A giant wave washes Kilala and Rei into the sea, where they discover the magical world of the Little Mermaid. Kilala tries to enjoy herself, but she's worried-- where is Rei?

JOIN KILALA AND THE DISNEY PRINCESSES FOR MORE ADVENTURES IN VOLUME 3!

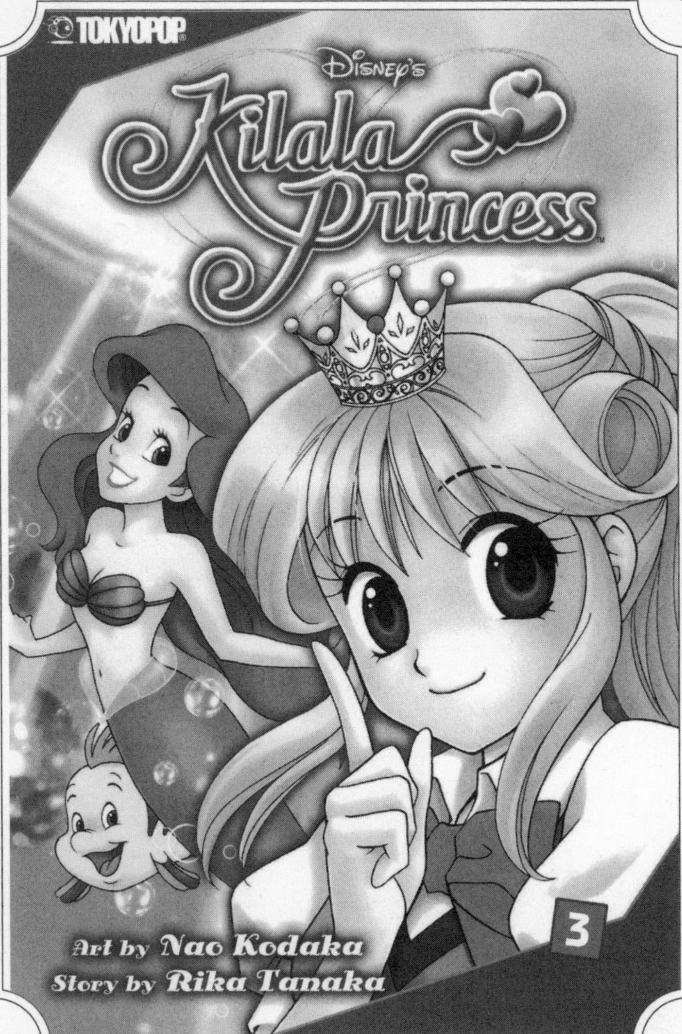
TOKYOPOP
Disney's
Kilala Princess
3
Art by Nao Kodaka
Story by Rika Tanaka

PRINCESS in Japanese

姫 means Princess in Japanese. It's pronounced "hime" ("hi" as in "heat" and "me" as in "melon")

Princess Aurora and Snow White are two princesses with "hime" in their name. Do you see where the character is?

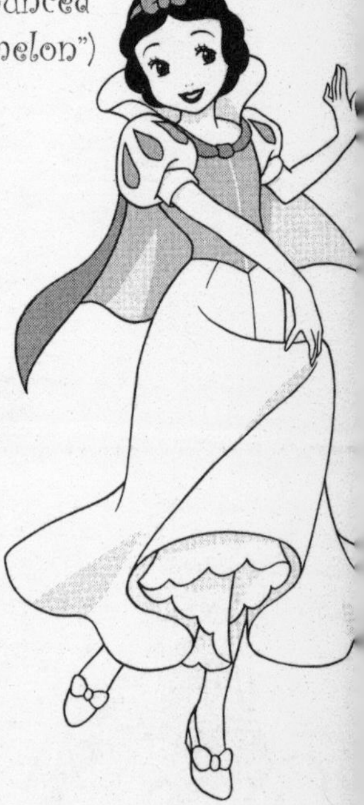

白雪姫

SNOW WHITE

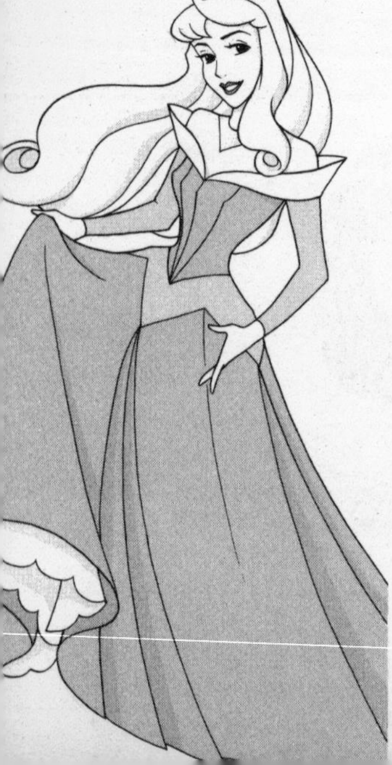

オーロラ姫

PRINCESS AURORA

You may not be able to tell by just looking at it, but this kanji (Chinese character) is actually composed of two parts!

女 and 臣

女 (onna) means "woman," while
臣 (jin) means "subject." A "woman subject" is a princess!

Other useful words the symbol of 女 appears in include:
娘 (musume) = daughter

What are women best at being?
嬉しい (ureshii) = happy

But, uh-oh, it's also in:
嫌い (kirai) = to hate

THANKS FOR READING!

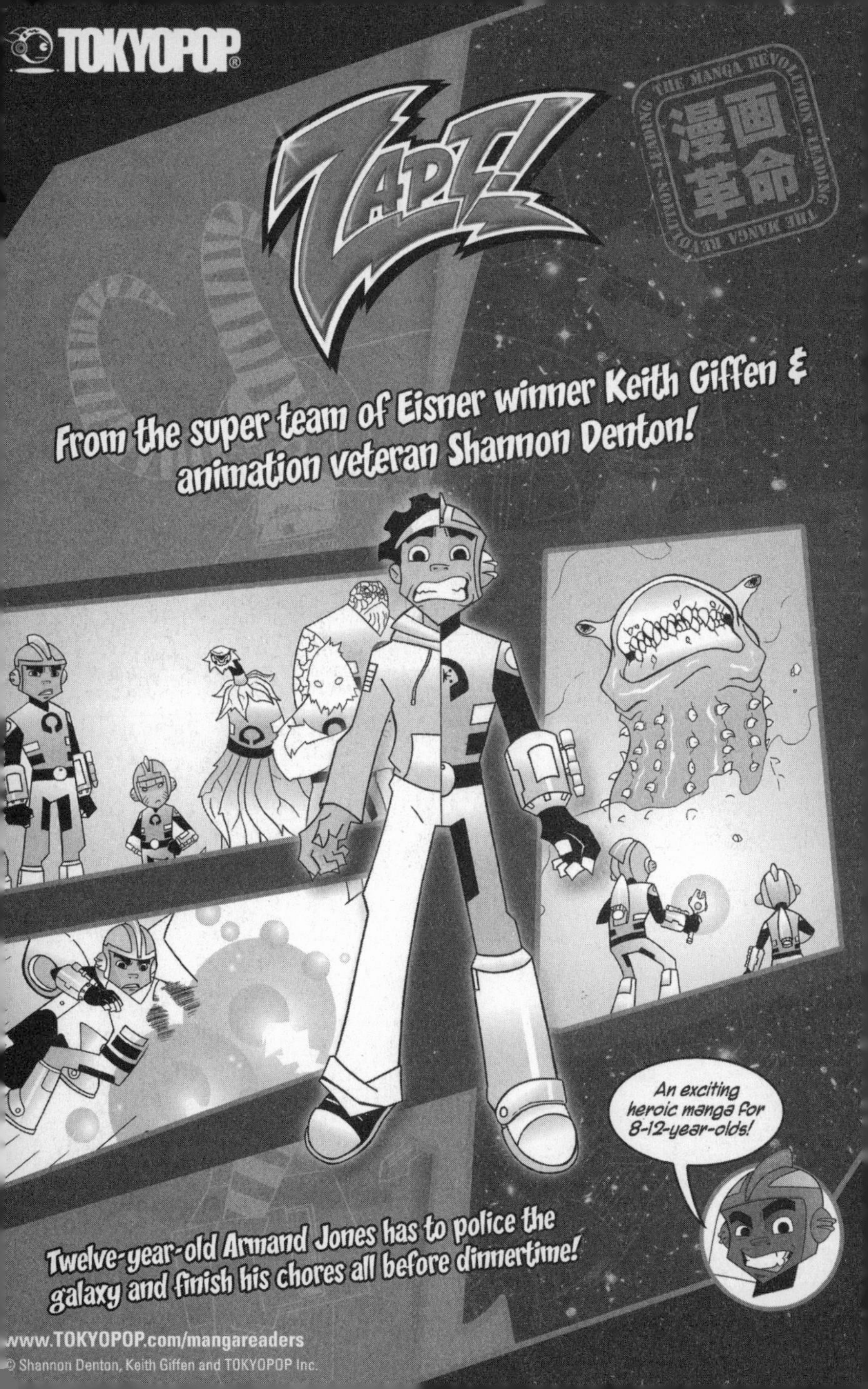
TOKYOPOP
ZAP!
THE MANGA REVOLUTION · LEADING
漫画革命
From the super team of Eisner winner Keith Giffen & animation veteran Shannon Denton!
An exciting heroic manga for 8-12-year-olds!
Twelve-year-old Armand Jones has to police the galaxy and finish his chores all before dinnertime!
www.TOKYOPOP.com/mangareaders
© Shannon Denton, Keith Giffen and TOKYOPOP Inc.

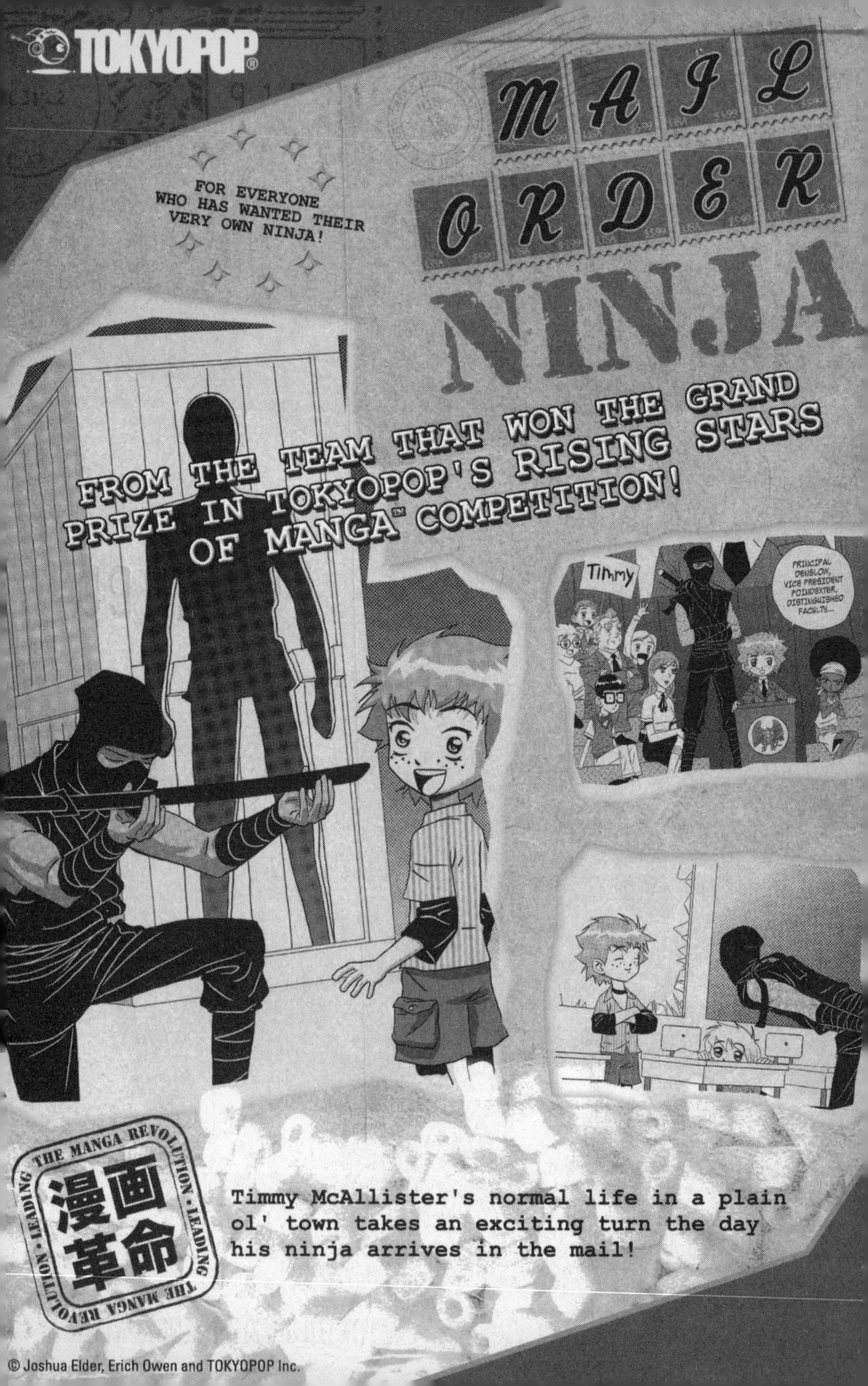
TOKYOPOP®
MAIL ORDER NINJA
FOR EVERYONE WHO HAS WANTED THEIR VERY OWN NINJA!
FROM THE TEAM THAT WON THE GRAND PRIZE IN TOKYOPOP'S RISING STARS OF MANGA™ COMPETITION!
Timmy
PRINCIPAL DENBLOW, VICE PRESIDENT POINDEXTER, DISTINGUISHED FACULTY...
THE MANGA REVOLUTION · LEADING · THE MANGA REVOLUTION · LEADING
漫画革命
Timmy McAllister's normal life in a plain ol' town takes an exciting turn the day his ninja arrives in the mail!
© Joshua Elder, Erich Owen and TOKYOPOP Inc.

Bonus Lab Experiment

Kat & mouse™

1 teacher torture

Story: Alex de Campi
Art: Federica Manfredi

When Kat moves to a posh private school, things seem perfect--that is, until a clique of rich, popular kids frame Kat's science teacher dad for stealing school property. Can Kat and her new friend, rebellious computer nerd Mouse, prove who the real culprits are before Kat's dad loses his job?

SPECIAL LOW MANGA PRICE: $5.99

A ALL AGES

PREVIEW THE MANGA FOR FREE: WWW.TOKYOPOP.COM/MANGAONLINE

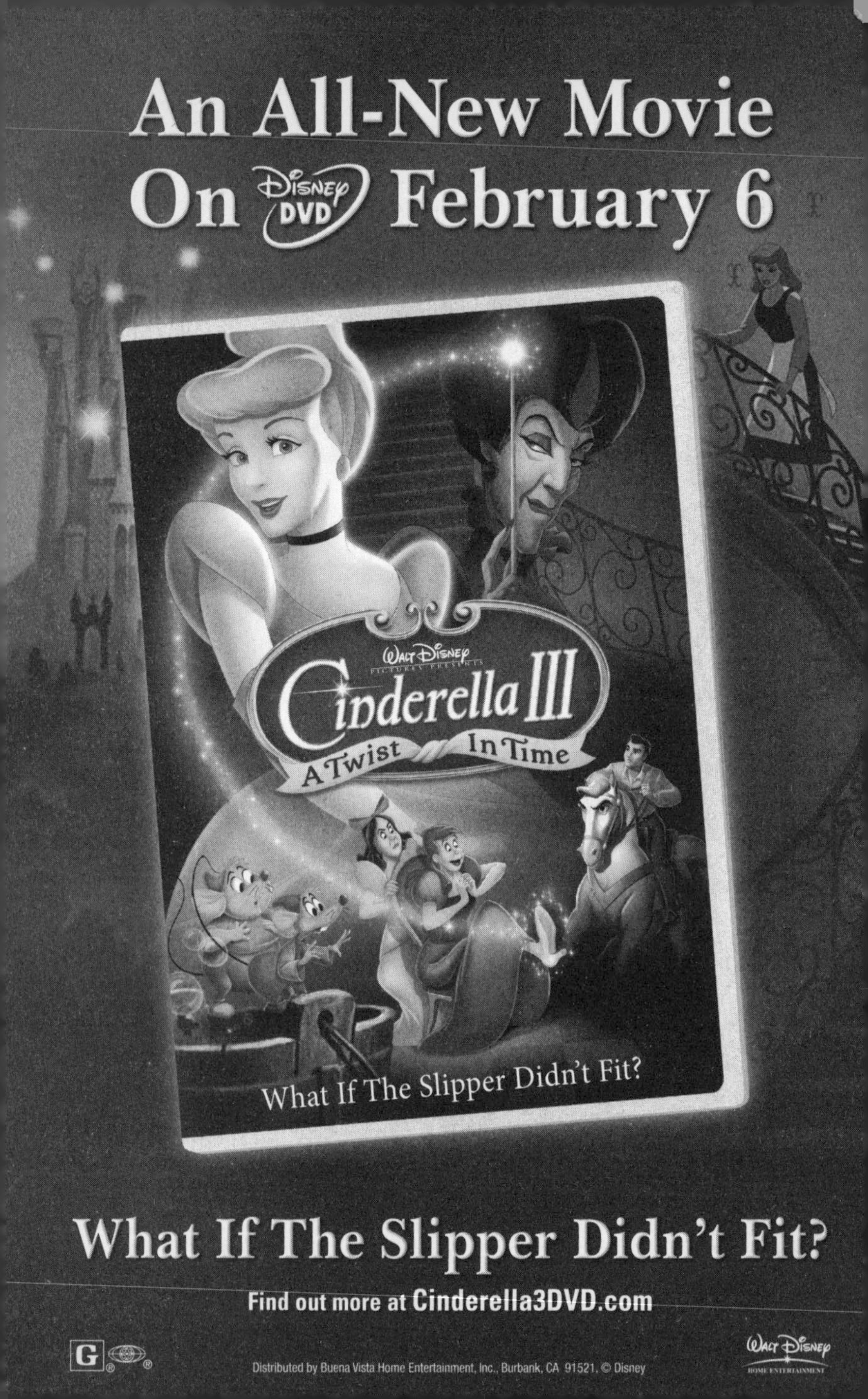
An All-New Movie
On Disney DVD February 6
Walt Disney Pictures Presents
Cinderella III
A Twist In Time
What If The Slipper Didn't Fit?
What If The Slipper Didn't Fit?
Find out more at Cinderella3DVD.com
G
Distributed by Buena Vista Home Entertainment, Inc., Burbank, CA 91521. © Disney
Walt Disney Home Entertainment

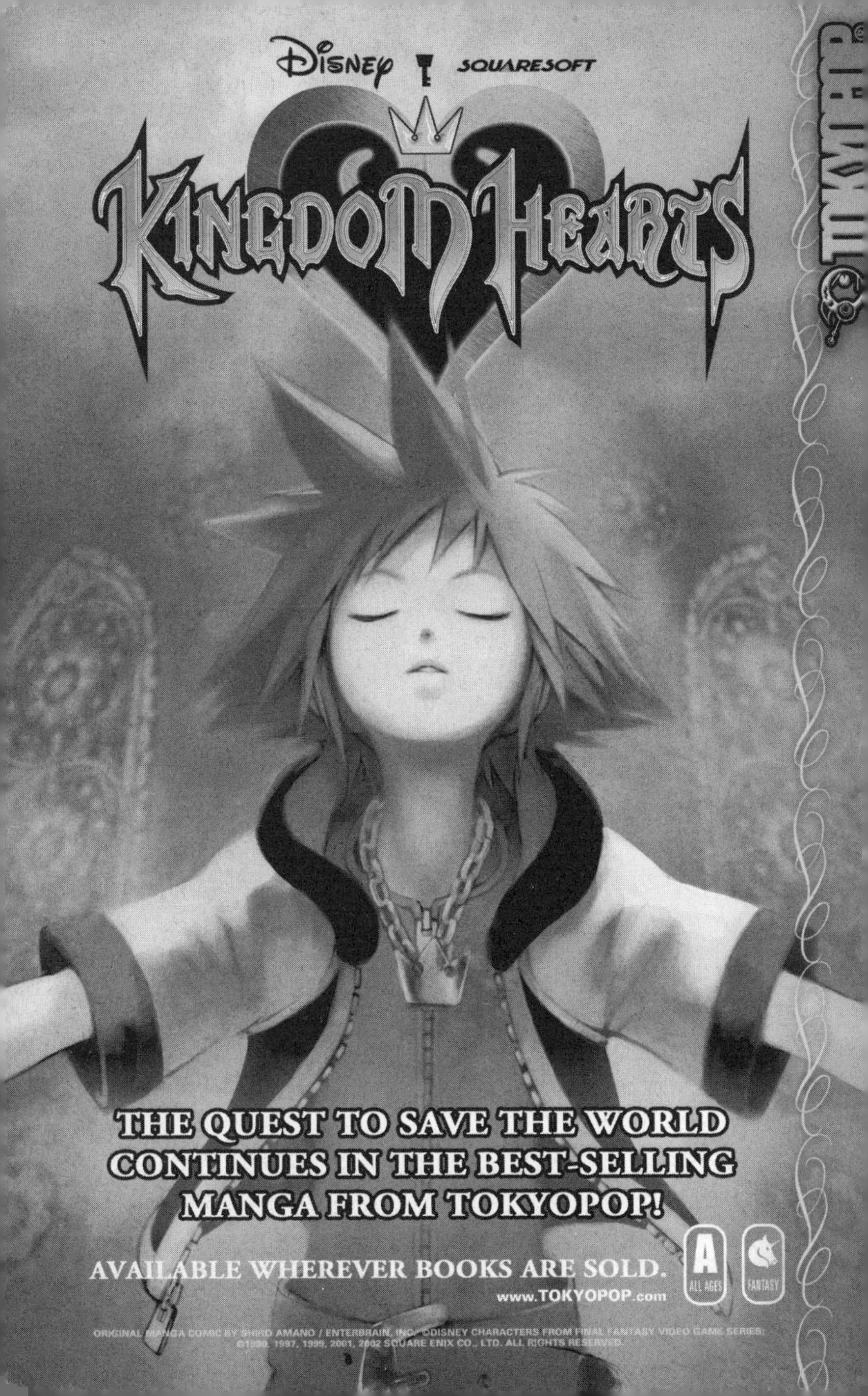

DISNEY
SQUARESOFT
KINGDOM HEARTS
TOKYOPOP
THE QUEST TO SAVE THE WORLD CONTINUES IN THE BEST-SELLING MANGA FROM TOKYOPOP!
AVAILABLE WHEREVER BOOKS ARE SOLD.
www.TOKYOPOP.com
A
ALL AGES
FANTASY
ORIGINAL MANGA COMIC BY SHIRO AMANO / ENTERBRAIN, INC. ©DISNEY CHARACTERS FROM FINAL FANTASY VIDEO GAME SERIES:
©1990, 1997, 1999, 2001, 2002 SQUARE ENIX CO., LTD. ALL RIGHTS RESERVED.

STOP

THIS IS THE BACK OF THE BOOK!

How do you read manga-style? It's simple! To learn, just start in the top right panel and follow the numbers:

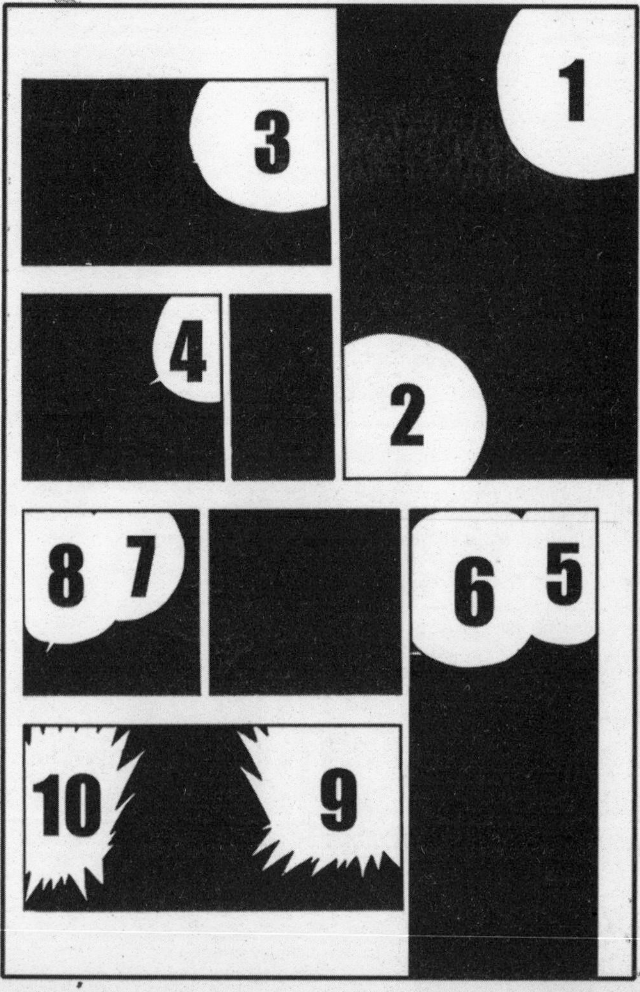

1
2
3
4
5
6
7
8
9
10